# CONTINUITY AND CHANGE IN THE SOCIAL COMPETENCE OF CHILDREN WITH AUTISM, DOWN SYNDROME, AND DEVELOPMENTAL DELAYS

*Marian Sigman and Ellen Ruskin*

**IN COLLABORATION WITH**
*Shoshana Arbelle*
*Rosalie Corona*
*Cheryl Dissanayake*
*Michael Espinosa*
*Norman Kim*
*Alma López*
*Cynthia Zierhut*

**WITH COMMENTARY BY**
*Carolyn B. Mervis*
*Byron F. Robinson*

**EDITOR**
*Rachel K. Clifton*

© 1999 Society for Research in Child Development

Blackwell Publishers, Inc.
350 Main Street
Malden, MA 02148 USA

Blackwell Publishers, Ltd.
108 Cowley Road
Oxford OX4 1JF
United Kingdom

All rights reserved. Except for the quotation of short passages for the purpose of criticism and review, no part of this publication may be reproduced, stored in a retrieval system, or transmitted in any form or by any means, electronic, mechanical, photocopying, recording, or otherwise, without the prior permission of the publisher.

0-63121-591-3
A CIP catalog record for this book is available
from the Library of Congress

This book is dedicated to Lisa Capps
whose contribution to the welfare of children will live forever.

| UNIVERSITY OF HERTFORDSHIRE WATFORD CAMPUS LRC WATFORD WD2 8AT |
| --- |
| BIB  0631215913 |
| CLASS  155 4 SOC |
| LOCATION  OUC |
| BARCODE  ULL  0507407 |

# CONTENTS

ABSTRACT    v

I. BACKGROUND AND GOALS OF THIS STUDY    1

II. STABILITY OF DIAGNOSIS AND INTELLIGENCE    11

III. NONVERBAL COMMUNICATION, PLAY, AND LANGUAGE SKILLS    29

IV. SOCIAL AND EMOTIONAL RESPONSIVENESS    54

V. PEER INTERACTIONS IN SCHOOL    66

VI. CORRELATES AND PREDICTORS OF PEER INTERACTIONS IN SCHOOL    88

VII. SUMMARY AND DISCUSSION    98

REFERENCES    109

ACKNOWLEDGMENTS    114

## COMMENTARY

METHODOLOGICAL ISSUES IN CROSS-SYNDROME COMPARISONS: MATCHING PROCEDURES, SENSITIVITY (*SE*), AND SPECIFICITY (*SP*)
*Carolyn B. Mervis and Byron F. Robinson*    115

RESPONSE TO THE COMMENTARY BY MERVIS AND ROBINSON
*Marian Sigman*    131

CONTRIBUTORS    140

# ABSTRACT

Marian Sigman and Ellen Ruskin. Continuity and Change in the Social Competence of Children With Autism, Down Syndrome, and Developmental Delays. With Commentary by Carolyn B. Mervis and Byron F. Robinson. *Monographs of the Society for Research in Child Development*, 1999, **64**(1, Serial No. 256).

The aims of this longitudinal study were: (1) to assess the continuity and change in diagnosis, intelligence, and language skills in children with autism, Down syndrome, and other developmental delays, (2) to specify the deficits in social competence and language skills in these children, and (3) to identify precursors in the preschool period of gains in language skills and of peer engagement in the mid-school years. The initial sample consisted of 70 children with autism, 93 children with Down syndrome, 59 children with developmental delays, and 108 typically developing children, with the first three groups of children studied when they were between 2 and 6 years of age. At follow-up, 51 children with autism, 71 children with Down syndrome, and 33 children with developmental delays were assessed at mean ages around 10–13 years. The long-term follow-up showed little change in the diagnosis of autism but sizeable improvements in intellectual and language abilities within the autistic group, a pattern that was not seen in the children with Down syndrome. Unique deficits in joint attention, some forms of representational play, responsiveness to the emotions of others, and initiation of peer engagement were identified in the autistic children, whereas the children with Down syndrome seemed to have a specific deficit only in language. Joint attention skills were concurrently associated with language abilities in all groups and predicted long-term gains in expressive language for the children with autism. Children with autism, regardless of their level of functioning, were less socially engaged with classmates than the other developmentally disabled children because they infrequently initiated and accepted play bids, not because they were rebuffed by peers. Early nonverbal communication and play skills were predictors of the frequency of initiations of peer play for the children with Down syndrome as well as the extent of peer engagement of the children with autism. These results suggest that improvements in early communication and play skills may have long-term consequences for later language and social competence in these groups of children.

# I. BACKGROUND AND GOALS OF THIS STUDY

The development of communicative and social competence over the childhood years is enormously important for all children. The achievement of optimal social competence is crucial for individuals with neurodevelopmental disorders, such as autism and Down syndrome. The extent to which these individuals are able to adjust to independent or semi-independent vocational and living settings depends to a great extent on their social skills. Adults with developmental delays are rejected from vocational settings more frequently because of their inability to get along with coworkers than because of their incapacities to fulfill work requirements. Similarly, the degree to which individuals with developmental delays can live independently is as much a function of their social skills as their cognitive abilities. Social responsiveness and emotional control are significant determinants of successful group living; given certain lower limits, level of intelligence is far less important.

Social competence also is critically important for individuals with neurodevelopmental disorders in that a rewarding social life can substitute for the professional achievements often foreclosed to the developmentally disabled. In working with families who have children with mental retardation, one is often impressed by the warmth, compassion, and humor that characterize their interactions. Families sometimes seem to be transformed by the presence of a handicapped child so that the focus on achievement and competition that often dominates family life is replaced by a concern for the emotional well-being of family members. The extent to which families are able to maintain this kind of concern depends partly on the characteristics of their handicapped child. Children who are socially responsive and self-controlled are able to contribute to family life in ways that are impossible for children who are either very isolated or explosive. Moreover, the social relationships that can be formed and maintained by the developmentally delayed individual as he or she matures depend to a very large extent on the level of the individual's social competence.

1

Given the importance of social competence in the lives of the developmentally delayed, there have been relatively few investigations of this critical ability. In addition, few longitudinal studies have been carried out and most of these have followed children for no more than a few years. For this reason, our understanding of the course of development of children with neurodevelopmental disorders is severely limited. While investigations of these children have increased in number in the last 20 to 30 years, most studies have been cross-sectional and restricted in scope to the investigation of cognitive abilities and achievements. With a few notable exceptions, the longitudinal studies that do exist are mainly follow-ups at later ages of clinical samples seen for assessment or intervention at earlier ages. Because the participants were seen as patients, the information collected on them originally was usually descriptive. If any early assessments were conducted, these generally were confined to such standardized measures as intelligence tests. Moreover, clinical studies have participants who vary considerably in age both at intake and follow-up. For this reason, we know very little about the extent of continuity or change that exists in the development of these children.

Limited information exists about the continuity of diagnosis and severity of symptoms as well as about the stability of intelligence in children with autism. Clinical follow-ups have been conducted in many countries to examine the quality of adjustment of the group in the adult years using a simple scale of life adjustment (Lotter, 1974). These studies show, with considerable unanimity, that the majority of adults with autism have very poor adaptive skills and many require considerable assistance with daily living. One very important finding from these studies is that children who have more advanced language skills by 5–6 years of age tend to have more successful life adaptations than children without such language skills (Rutter, 1970). Studies by Catherine Lord and her collaborators (Lord & Venter, 1992; Venter, Lord, & Schopler, 1992) indicate that intelligence stays stable for autistic children as a group, although there is more change when the children with autism are recruited and tested in the preschool years (Lord & Schopler, 1989a). Very little has been established empirically about continuity of diagnosis because standardized measures of assessment have been available only for about the last 8–10 years.

A somewhat larger number of longitudinal studies has been conducted of children with Down syndrome than of children with autism, most likely because of the ease of diagnosis and the greater number of participants available at any site. Many longitudinal studies follow the children for only a few years and focus on specific domains such as temperament (Vaughn, Contreras, & Seifer, 1994), language acquisition (Mervis, 1988; Tager-Flusberg, 1986), or adaptive skills (Dykens, Hodapp, & Evans, 1994; Loveland & Kelley, 1988; Sloper & Turner, 1996). Many longer term studies have shown that there is a decline in the rate of mental development with increasing age in children with Down syndrome (for example, Carr, 1988; Piper, Gendron, & Mazer, 1986; Rauh et al., 1991; Wishart & Duffy, 1990).

The aim of the research program described in this monograph is to define deficits in the skills of children with autism and Down syndrome and to identify the impact of variations in these skills on their concurrent and future development of language and social competence. In addition, the research also examines continuity and change in the diagnosis of autism and mental retardation as well as the stability of intelligence and linguistic skills over time. A developmental perspective informs this research so that the concepts and methods used to investigate these disabilities are drawn from the study of normal development and the results of the studies inform our understanding of both typical and disabled children.

## CONCEPTUAL BACKGROUND FOR THE PROGRAM OF RESEARCH

The organizing principles that underlie this research program come from theoretical conceptions that emphasize the importance of interpersonal communication and symbolic representation for the development of children (Bruner, 1975; Werner & Kaplan, 1963). Language acquisition is thought to require that the child have some capacity for symbolic representation (Piaget, 1952) as well as communicative intentions (Bates, Benigni, Bretherton, Camaioni, & Volterra, 1979; Vygotsky, 1978). In support of these conceptions, studies of typically developing children have shown that the emergence of symbolic play skills is paralleled by advances in language. Moreover, a developmental sequence in social responsiveness and understanding has been documented in which dyadic interaction at 4 to 6 months of age is supplemented some 6 to 10 months later by triadic interactions in which infant and partner begin to attend conjointly to inanimate objects or other people (Adamson & Bakeman, 1985; Bretherton, 1991; Tomasello, 1997). This triadic interaction pattern indexes the emerging understanding of the infant that other people have independent viewpoints that can be shared and is associated with the growth of receptive language. The achievements in symbolic representation and communicative intent stem from the infant's developing mental capacities as well as from affective experiences that both drive and intensify these achievements. With language acquisition, there is a reorganization in both the conceptual and social world of the infant. Children may fail to acquire language skills because of limitations in the symbolic and social precursors of language. Limited language skills, in turn, intensify the difficulties in the symbolic and social realms that were already present.

The goal of our research program was to apply this framework to both children with autism and children with Down syndrome. Severe limitations in language have been identified in individuals with autism, with about half unable to use any productive language (DeMyer et al., 1973; Eisenberg, 1956; Rutter & Lockyer, 1967). Given these severe limitations in language acquisition, we expected that the development of representational play and nonverbal communication would be compromised in many children with autism. Some early studies had reported that children with autism did not show age-appropriate symbolic play although these studies did not use observational systems based on known developmental sequences nor were there comparisons of play skills with those of matched control participants. To our knowledge, there were no studies of nonverbal communication when our research was first planned although one report of deficits in pointing in four autistic children (Curcio, 1978), was published soon afterward. Our guiding hypothesis at the start of this research program was that children with autism would have deficits in representational play and nonverbal communication and that variations in these abilities would be important for their acquisition of language.

When this research program was begun and for many years after, sample sizes and funding were too small to allow for linkages to be made to social competence in other settings, and only short-term (1-year) follow-ups were conducted. The continuous recruitment and testing of participants over many years resulted in sufficient sample sizes to allow a longer-term longitudinal follow-up so that predictive links to later language skills and social competence could be examined. The guiding hypothesis for the follow-up of the children with autism was that early nonverbal communication and representational play skills would have long-term consequences for their subsequent language gains and social competence with peers and that the links between early communication and play with later social competence would be somewhat independent of early language skills.

Our conceptualizations regarding the development of children with Down syndrome were less fully drawn. Children with Down syndrome also were known to have language problems but the difficulties were less severe in that most children were able to understand and use language to some extent (Fowler, 1995; Miller & Chapman, 1984). Furthermore, the research and clinical literature and our early observations suggested that children with Down syndrome were socially communicative and capable of imaginary play. For this reason, our examination of group differences in representational play and nonverbal communication was more exploratory and less hypothesis driven than was true for our studies of autistic children. Early nonverbal communication and symbolic skills were expected to be associated with concurrent language skills and short-term gains in language, as had been shown in the research literature on typical developing children. Later language acquisition and competence with peers, however, was expected to be only moderately predicted by early communicative and play skills because of the relative skillfulness of the children with Down syndrome. A major question of the follow-up study was the extent to which the children with Down syndrome differed from children with heterogeneous developmental delays in terms of their social competence with peers. Moreover, we wished to know whether the high level of social interest shown by some young children with Down syndrome was advantageous to their later development.

## PREVIOUS RESEARCH RESULTS

The current study grew out of two research programs, one an investigation of the development of children with autism and the second an investigation of the development of children with Down syndrome. The autism project was begun in 1979 with a cross-sectional investigation of the cognitive and language skills of children with autism. The object knowledge of young autistic children was found to be relatively intact in contrast to their symbolic skills as manifested in play and language (Sigman & Ungerer, 1981; Sigman & Ungerer, 1984; Ungerer & Sigman, 1981). A second study with newly recruited participants extended these findings by identifying a deficiency in nonverbal communication, specific to the autistic sample. Three components of nonverbal communication were studied: (1) joint attention, defined as sharing of attention to objects or interesting events, (2) behavior regulation, manifested in the child's actions aimed at requesting of objects or assistance with objects, and (3) social interactions (Bruner & Sherwood, 1983). The children with autism were much less likely to initiate or respond to joint attention with either the experimenter or a parent than control participants, although they were as likely to interact socially and to attempt to regulate the behavior of others in order to obtain certain objects or experiences (Mundy, Sigman, Ungerer, & Sherman, 1986; Sigman, Mundy, Sherman, & Ungerer, 1986). The third study in this sequence replicated these results with newly recruited samples (Mundy, Sigman, & Kasari, 1994) and also showed that children with autism were relatively inattentive to the faces of other people even when these people showed strong emotions (Sigman, Kasari, Kwon, & Yirmiya, 1992).

All the aforementioned studies included not only young children with autism, generally between 3–6 years of age, but also control groups of children comprised equally of children with Down syndrome and with other forms of mental retardation. In our second study, our observation that the small group of control participants with Down syndrome were less likely to request objects or assistance with objects than was true for the normal group led us to extend the samples (Mundy, Sigman, Kasari, & Yirmiya, 1988). This deficit in behavior regulation was found with this extended sample and with newly recruited samples in a subsequent study (Mundy, Kasari, Sigman, &

Ruskin, 1995). Moreover, the replication study showed that language skills were somewhat higher in children with Down syndrome who made more use of nonverbal behavior regulation than those who did so less or not at all. The use of requesting gestures by the children with Down syndrome sample was predictive of gains in language skills in a 1-year follow-up of the sample.

Most of the studies described above included 1-year longitudinal follow-ups. The sample size in each of these longitudinal follow-ups was small because the numbers recruited in each cross-sectional study ranged from 16 to 42 children in a group. The total number of children involved in all our studies conducted since 1979, however, is considerable. The current investigation was designed to take advantage of the availability of the relatively large number of children with autism, Down syndrome, and other forms of mental retardation and developmental delay who have been followed in our research program, starting from the time that they were 2–6 years of age.

## GOALS OF THE CURRENT STUDY

### Identification of Continuity and Change in Diagnosis and Level of Intelligence

At the broadest level, the extent to which children recover partly or fully from developmental disorders is critically important. Surprisingly, there is limited information about continuity and change in disorders because standardized diagnostic measures have only recently been formulated and used. Moreover, with autism, problems in measuring continuity and change in diagnosis continue to exist. Because most individuals are diagnosed fairly early in childhood and never rediagnosed, diagnostic measures focus on the positive and negative symptoms that occur in early childhood. This focus on early symptoms also is required by one of the criteria for diagnosis, the emergence of the disorder before the age of 3 years. Given that diagnostic instruments aim to determine whether the child suffered from the disorder in the past, there is less assessment of current symptomatology so that it is difficult to compare symptoms across time. In this study, we have examined changes in diagnosis using parental reports of current symptoms in both children originally diagnosed with autism and those diagnosed with diverse developmental disorders.

One child characteristic that has been investigated in depth is intelligence. As mentioned above, stability seems moderately high once children with autism and Down syndrome have reached school age, a finding also true for typically developing children. There is less stability when children are tracked from the preschool period for both children with autism and those with Down syndrome. This study examines both group and individual stability in children with autism and Down syndrome in contrast to those who have more heterogeneous developmental disorders.

### Reexamination of Deficits in Symbolic Play, Social Communication, and Emotional Responsiveness in Larger Samples Than Were Previously Available

In past studies, we have identified deficits in young children (age 3–5 years) with autism in symbolic play, nonverbal communication, and responsiveness to the distress of others, and in nonverbal communication in young children with Down syndrome. We have lacked the information, however, to determine whether these deficits are specific, universal, and unique to these syndromes. Specificity refers to the extent of disabilities. Children who are similarly delayed in all domains cannot be said to suffer from specific deficits. In order to establish specificity, several abilities or behaviors of children with a neurodevelopmental syndrome are compared with the same abilities or behaviors of children who are similar in overall intelligence or language skills. Only in those cases where a single ability or set of abilities is affected can one really speak of specific deficits. For example, evidence will be presented later in this monograph suggesting that children with Down syndrome have deficits specific to language acquisition in that their nonverbal communication and symbolic play skills are not impaired.

Universality refers to the extent that the deficit is shared by the children who suffer from the syndrome. This characteristic can only be determined by investigations of children who vary in terms of their age, developmental level, and severity of symptoms. In order for a deficit to be truly characteristic of a syndrome, all children who suffer from the syndrome must be limited in the same skill or characteristic to some extent. If some portion of the sample does not suffer from the same disability, the deficit cannot be considered characteristic of the syndrome unless there is some explanation for the compensation of this subsample for their potential or former limitations. With development, the abilities and characteristics of children may change so that previous deficits may be overcome. An example of such a change is the increasing sociability with age of some children with autism. At the same time, these children continue to appear socially naive and to manifest less understanding of their peers and themselves.

Uniqueness refers to the extent to which a deficit or pattern of deficits characterizes one or more than one syndrome. Thus, if executive function deficits are found in children with autism, schizophrenic children, and children with attention-deficit hyperactive disorder (ADHD), then executive function deficits are not unique to autism unless some more narrowly defined form of executive function deficit is identified. Because there are limitations to the number of abilities or characteristics that can be disturbed

7

without threatening the individual's viability, similar disabilities are likely to characterize the functioning of children who suffer from a variety of syndromes. Uniqueness is the most difficult characteristic to assess because of the impossibility of studying all the relevant syndromes.

The investigation of the specificity, universality, and uniqueness of deficits can only be accomplished by the assessment of numerous child abilities as well as diverse groups of children with a variety of syndromes. The availability of our aggregated data set allows us in this monograph to investigate the specificity, universality, and uniqueness of deficits more precisely than has been possible with our more limited data in the past. In addition, more powerful analyses of the concurrent associations between nonverbal communication and play skills with verbal abilities can be conducted for each group than was previously possible with smaller samples.

## Specification of Deficits in Social Competence
## in Older Children With Autism and Down Syndrome

Another goal of this study is to identify skills and deficits in social competence in the children at an older age (10–12 years) by comparing their emotional responsiveness to adults in a laboratory setting and their peer interactions in school. School-age children with autism (particularly low functioning children) and children with Down syndrome have been studied much less than younger children. For this reason, there are few studies of the social behavior of these children either with adults or, more importantly, with their classmates. Thus, a major aim of this study was to describe the pattern of interactions shown by these children on the school playground and in the classroom.

As discussed above, the specification of deficits and skills for any diagnostic group depends on comparisons of the behaviors of children in that group with children in control groups. These control groups need to be of similar mental abilities and chronological ages. Control for mental or language abilities is imperative because most of the children in the groups studied suffer from some degree of mental and language retardation. A comparison of the social competence of children of very different mental or language abilities would not be interpretable. Chronological age has to be considered, particularly for children over 5 years of age, because the experiences available to children in any society are determined to a very large extent by their ages. For this reason, comparisons of children who differ widely in age may reflect this variation in living situations and experiences rather than differences in their abilities and characteristics.

The previously described studies of 2- to 6-year-old children that we have conducted have included two control groups, one comprised of developmentally disabled children including some with Down syndrome, and the other comprised of typically developing children, matched on language abilities but not on chronological age. In the follow-up study, the typically developing control group was not studied for several reasons. First, we could not use the samples collected previously because they would no longer have the same mental or language abilities as the mentally retarded groups. While normal children advance about 1 year in 1 year's time, developmentally delayed children advance more like 4–6 months in 1 year's time. Our longitudinal follow-up was conducted about 8 years after the original study. Given the different rates of development, the developmentally disabled and normal groups who were originally matched on mental age would now have a mental age discrepancy of about 6 years.

The second reason for excluding a normal control group is that the experiences of children diversify more as they age. Ten- to twelve-year-old mentally retarded children are likely to be in classrooms and after-school activities that differ a great deal from the classrooms and activities of the three- to five-year-old normal children with whom they would match on mental abilities. The comparison of social interactions in these very dissimilar school settings would be difficult to interpret as group differences might be attributable to these differences in school settings rather than characteristics or abilities. For this reason, a typically developing group was not studied in the follow-up investigation and the comparisons are between groups differing in diagnosis but similar in mental and language abilities and chronological age.

### Identification of the Components of Social Competence in Children With Autism and Down Syndrome

The identification of components of social competence and how these interrelate for each group of children is another aim of this study. Competence in handling social interactions and adjusting to social situations requires a number of abilities and proclivities for any individual. These abilities are not always easy to distinguish or to measure. There is value, however, in attempting to differentiate between the components of social life in order to understand where problems exist and interventions are required. For the purposes of this study, we decompose social competence into three components: (1) *communicative abilities*, (2) *responsiveness to others' emotions and needs*, and (3) *peer interactions*. We have defined and operationalized these components based on what is known about social competence in the research literature and acknowledge that different definitions and measurement techniques could be implemented. The components we examined, however, were selected to be relevant to these populations as well as measurable with the majority of the participants in the study. An important component of social competence is social understanding, but this was difficult to assess in many children in this sample because of their very limited language skills. One

9

issue to be explored is the extent to which each component is associated with general cognitive abilities, whereas a second purpose is to identify the extent to which communicative abilities and social responsiveness are associated with peer engagement in each group.

### Determination of the Precursors of Verbal Communicative Skills and Social Competence in Children With Autism and Down Syndrome

The final goal of this study is to identify the precursors of social competence in each of these groups. The identification of precursors of verbal communicative and social skills may be of particular significance for the design of early intervention programs. As an example, the identification of joint attention skills in 2- to 5-year-old children as a precursor of language skills measured 1 year later has led some intervention programs to attempt to improve the joint attention skills of young autistic children.

It should be noted that the abilities and characteristics that can be studied in the current follow-up depend on what was selected for study when the children were younger. Moreover, the children in this follow-up study were originally recruited into five different studies, all with different aims and, therefore, employing different methods. For this reason, there is variation in the number of children within each sample who have been administered each of the early measures. Most of the children were administered similar developmental and language measures. In addition, many of the children were administered early assessments of play and nonverbal communication skills because of our continuing interest in these areas of functioning.

In summary, the overall purpose of this monograph is to examine change and continuity in the diagnosis and intelligence levels of children with autism and Down syndrome, to define deficits in the social competence of these children, and to identify precursors of school-age social competence. Development was studied longitudinally not only in the laboratory but also in the school. Our primary goal is to specify domains that could possibly serve as targets for intervention programs aimed to optimize the functioning of these children as they progress through the school years.

# II. STABILITY OF DIAGNOSIS AND INTELLIGENCE

Life circumstances and adjustment vary with the level of development of the individual, whether the individual be a normal child or adult or a disabled individual. For example, very young children's social interactions usually are supervised by an adult or older sibling, whereas older children are expected to be able to handle themselves independently in social interactions with peers. For an individual with a neurodevelopmental disorder, life setting depends to a certain extent on their cognitive abilities. The level of social skills that can be acquired is partly a function of cognitive abilities so that individuals with very compromised intellects necessarily have limitations in their social abilities. Whereas social competence has other determinants besides cognitive competence, as pointed out in the introduction to this monograph, the relation between the two is strong enough to require that cognitive skills must be considered in any investigation of social competence.

For this reason, the monograph begins with an examination of the cognitive skills of the children in the sample. Besides providing a description of the sample, this chapter also will address several questions about stability over time of diagnosis and intelligence. An important issue for caregivers and educators is the extent to which children are able to recover from handicapping conditions. This issue will be addressed in two different ways. First, the stability of the diagnoses of autism and mental retardation will be examined. Second, the extent to which there is continuity or change in levels of intelligence over time will be described.

As discussed in the previous chapter, there have been relatively few long-term longitudinal studies of children with autism. Several investigators have examined a group of autistic children in early childhood and followed them into early or late adolescence, generally with only one follow-up visit, therefore affording comparison of abilities at just two points in time. These studies suggest that individuals with autism remain as severely affected by the disorder in adolescence as in childhood (Cantwell, Baker, Rutter, & Mawhood, 1989; Chung, Luk, & Lee, 1990; Eisenberg, 1956; Gillberg & Steffenburg, 1987; Goldfarb, 1970; Hindley & Owen, 1978; Kanner, 1971; Lord &

Schopler, 1989b; Lotter, 1978; Mittler, Gilles, & Jukes, 1966; Venter et al., 1992). As demonstrated by Lord and Schopler (1989a), autistic children's level of intelligence and language abilities stayed relatively stable through adolescence, particularly after correcting for the language delay associated with autism. Longer-range testing revealed less stability in intelligence for children who were tested in preschool and followed into adolescence and adulthood. A significant number of children who scored in the mild to moderately retarded range on IQ tests as preschoolers later performed in the nonretarded range on nonverbal and performance tests.

Follow-up studies of children with Down syndrome originally assessed during late infancy or the preschool period show a different pattern, with a decline in intelligence with age. For example, Janet Carr (1988) followed a group of 54 children with Down syndrome from 1½ months of age with five assessments until 2 years and subsequent evaluations at 3, 4, 11, and 21 years. Mean developmental quotients on the Bayley Scale fell from 80 at 6 months to 45 at 4 years with a further decline to 37 at 11 years. More recent studies (Piper et al., 1986; Rauh et al., 1991; Wishart & Duffy, 1990) show similar patterns of decline in developmental rate even though intervention programs have been effective in helping children to achieve skills at earlier ages.

Given the previous findings, we expected that the majority of children diagnosed as autistic would remain so at follow-up and that children in the other groups would not develop autism as they matured. Furthermore, considerable stability was expected in intelligence for each group as a whole. Based on the previous findings, however, it seemed possible that the children with autism might show somewhat less individual stability in intelligence than the other children and that the children with Down syndrome would show a decline in intelligence.

## ORIGINAL RECRUITMENT AND SELECTION OF PARTICIPANTS

Children who had been identified by a clinician with a diagnosis of autism, Down syndrome, or suspected developmental delay were recruited into the original studies. The recruitment sources and methods differed for the varying diagnostic groups and are described below in the following four sections.

### Children With Autism

The locations for recruiting participants varied over the course of the study because of the trend away from inpatient hospitalization to outpatient treatment that occurred in our institution, the Neuropsychiatric Institute at the University of California, Los Angeles (UCLA), as well as the rest of the country. When we started our first study, children with autism and other developmental disorders were hospitalized routinely for 3 to 6 months so that the first half of our sample of children with autism was recruited while on our inpatient unit. Like other hospitals in the United States, inpatient hospitalization for childhood psychopathology became more infrequent and lengths of inpatient stays declined in our ward. As this occurred, we had little time to see children while they were on the ward. For this reason, the second half of the autistic sample were outpatients, although many of the children who were included in this sample had been inpatients briefly at one time.

In addition to the movement from studying inpatients to outpatients, the methods for diagnosing children with autism changed over the course of the study. These changes were made partly as a function of this alteration in treatment patterns and as a function of international changes in research and clinical practice. For autism as well as other forms of psychopathology, standardized interviews and observations began to replace clinical diagnoses in research studies. Similarly, we moved from sole reliance on clinician's diagnoses, based on standards for diagnosis set forth in DSM III (American Psychiatric Association, 1980) or III-R (American Psychiatric Association, 1987), to the combined use of clinicians' diagnoses, standardized observations, and interviews. The first half of the 70 children with autism seen in these studies were diagnosed by clinicians on the inpatient unit in the Neuropsychiatric Institute or by a special diagnostic team that was part of the Center for Research on Childhood Psychosis. Diagnoses were formulated by interdisciplinary teams of clinicians who had extensive experience with childhood psychopathology. In addition, the children were well known to the clinicians making the diagnoses because of their lengthy hospital stays.

The second half of the sample also had clinical diagnoses but these were frequently made by a single clinician. These clinical diagnoses were supplemented with diagnoses based on two other sources, a videotaped observation scored with the Childhood Autism Rating Scale (CARS; Schopler, Reichler, & Renner, 1986), and an interview during which the Autism Behavior Checklist (ABC; Krug, Arick, & Almond, 1980) was administered to the parents. Only children who met the cutoffs for diagnosis of autism on at least two of these three methods—the clinical diagnosis, CARS, and ABC—were included in the sample of children with autism.

## Children With Down Syndrome

Ninety-three children with Down syndrome were recruited from school programs and from local parents' groups. We obtained permission from the

13

Los Angeles School District to recruit from classrooms for 2 to 4-year-old children enrolled in school programs in all parts of the city. As the district does not offer schooling to typically developing children of this age, these classes tended to be for children with developmental delays. Some mainstreamed children also were recruited from preschools located during our efforts at recruiting normal children. Another major source of participants were parent groups, such as the Parents of Children with Down Syndrome Group, who allowed us to attend their meetings in order to describe the study and advertised our study in their newsletters. Down syndrome children remained in the study even if they did not test in the mentally retarded range on the developmental assessment.

### Children With Developmental Delays

Developmentally delayed children were recruited from all the sources reported above. The purpose of recruiting and studying this sample was to furnish information about a group of children of comparable chronological age and mental and language abilities to the children with autism and Down syndrome. Typically developing children can never be matched in this way because they will always be different either in chronological age or in mental and language abilities. The aim was to locate a heterogeneous group of children with various developmental delays and disorders; a homogeneous group would not serve the purpose as well, because such a group might have specific characteristics of its own. The only hypotheses that we formulated about this group were those that we thought to be applicable to all children in the sample. Thus, we did not expect that the developmentally delayed group would have particular deficits in nonverbal communication and representational play. On the other hand, we expected that those children with more advanced nonverbal communication and play skills would have better concurrent language skills. The extent to which communication and play skills would predict later language gains and social competence was not evident from any theoretical or empirical evidence available at the time that the hypotheses were formulated.

The first half of the sample were children with developmental delays hospitalized on the inpatient unit who were selected because autism was ruled out as a diagnosis. Changes in hospitalization practices made it less possible to locate developmentally delayed children on the inpatient unit, so the second half of the sample were recruited from outpatient services or schools in the community. Although it might seem that the first half of the sample would have more serious behavior problems than the second half, this is not clearly true because developmentally delayed children with only mild to moderate problems were frequently hospitalized for short periods on our inpatient units before hospitalization practices changed.

Only children who fulfilled the criteria for diagnosis on one or fewer of the diagnostic measures—the ABC administered to their parents in an interview, the CARS, and the clinical diagnosis—were included in this sample. Three children were diagnosed by clinicians as autistic but did not meet the criteria for autism on the ABC and the CARS, so they were retained in the developmentally delayed sample. A few of the children had developmental delays as part of a neurological syndrome such as Prader-Willi or resulting from severe birth complications, some had mental retardation with no identified cause, and some had mild to moderate language delays. Throughout this monograph, this group will be referred to as "developmentally delayed," although the children have problems that are long-standing. The term "developmentally disabled" is used in this monograph to refer to all the children with any form of disability in contrast to the "typically developing" or "normal" children.

### Typically Developing Children

This group of children were recruited from pediatric clinics at UCLA as well as local schools and youth activities. Developmental and language assessments were used to rule out developmental delays. The parents of the last third of the normal sample were administered the ABC and their tapes were scored with the CARS. No child recruited into the typically developing sample has ever been diagnosed with autism or any other developmental disability.

### Age at Initial Assessment

The general aim in recruitment was to find and test children who were as young as possible. For the children with autism, the limiting factor was age of identification and diagnosis. Very few children were diagnosed with autism earlier than 2½ years of age and most were not diagnosed and referred until 3–6 years of age. The first groups of children with Down syndrome and developmental delay were selected to match the autism group on chronological age so they also ranged in age from 3–6 years. The last study conducted of children with Down syndrome, however, recruited younger children. This was done because we wanted to identify preverbal children with Down syndrome who were motorically mature enough to be testable with our procedures. Thus, the age range for this sample was 1–3 years, younger than the previously tested samples. Because of this, the mean age at intake for the children with Down syndrome was about 2½ years, whereas it was closer to 4 years for

TABLE 1

DESCRIPTIVE INFORMATION ABOUT THE ORIGINAL SAMPLE AT INTAKE

| | | Autistic Group - 1 $n = 70$ | Down Syndrome Group - 2 $n = 93$ | Developmental Delay Group - 3 $n = 59$ | Normal Group - 4 $n = 108$ | Group Differences* |
|---|---|---|---|---|---|---|
| Chronological | Mean | 47.24 | 31.38 | 44.92 | 19.49 | 4 2 3 1 |
| Age** | SD | 12.14 | 13.67 | 15.11 | 8.00 | |
| Mental Age | Mean | 23.71 | 20.59 | 27.93 | 23.06 | 2 4 1 3 |
| | SD | 9.81 | 7.59 | 11.28 | 10.33 | |
| Developmental | Mean | 49.31 | 67.19 | 60.34 | 115.61 | 1 3 2 4 |
| Quotient | SD | 13.27 | 16.78 | 18.58 | 12.49 | |
| Language Age | Mean | 16.60 | 18.32 | 20.39 | 20.94 | 1 2 3 4 |
| | SD | 7.64 | 5.91 | 10.80 | 10.53 | |

*Means not joined by a line are significantly different from each other, $p < .05$.
**All ages are shown in months.

the other samples. Of course, the typically developing group was younger because of the need to match them to the other samples on mental and language abilities. (See Table 1 for descriptive data on the initial sample.)

### Intelligence Level and Mental Age

Initially, intelligence was assessed with the Cattell Scales of Development because this was the assessment procedure used in the clinical services in 1979 in the Department of Psychiatry at UCLA when these studies were begun and because the Cattell Scales were designed to extend upward to the Stanford-Binet (Thorndike, 1972). This version of the Stanford-Binet, which was the intelligence test most widely used with young children at the time this research program was originated, was administered to the higher functioning children who reached ceiling levels in performance on the Cattell scale. Both assessments furnish an estimate of mental age and either a Development Quotient (DQ) or Intelligence Quotient (IQ) for each subject. The majority of participants were administered the Cattell Scales (195 out of the 222 developmentally disordered children who were tested). Twenty-seven participants were administered the Stanford-Binet, five in the autistic group, four in the Down syndrome group, and eighteen in the developmentally delayed group. All the typically developing children were tested with the Cattell Scales.

The mean mental ages at time of first assessment ranged from 21 to 28 months for the four groups of children (see Table 1). The mean DQ/IQs of the groups varied, with the autistic sample at 49, the Down syndrome sample at 67, and the developmentally delayed sample at 60. The majority of children with autism were mentally retarded; only five had DQ/IQs of 70 or above, the traditional cutoff score for mental retardation. In contrast, about 43% of the children with Down syndrome had DQ/IQs of 70 or above. The developmentally delayed group was composed of 38 mentally retarded children and 21 children who had IQs above 69.

## RECRUITMENT OF PARTICIPANTS FOR THE SOCIAL COMPETENCE STUDY

The aim of the current recruitment was to locate and assess as many of the participants from the previous studies as possible. The sample was limited to children between 6 and 19 years old, because the settings for school observations were likely to be different below and above this age level. Because of this age limit, three participants who had reached their twenties, one with Down syndrome and two with developmental delays, were excluded, leaving the potential sample at 219 children.

Recruitment and testing of the sample began in December 1992 and ended in June 1996. The general strategy was to locate and test participants starting with the oldest participants and progressing downward in age in order to minimize the variation in time from last testing and to reach the participants when they were between 6 and 19 years old. Location of participants was accomplished by using their original telephone numbers and addresses, the numbers and addresses of nearest relatives, and information from schools, regional centers, and parents' groups. In the latter cases, parents were contacted and asked for permission for us to call them.

Parents were asked to come to our laboratory at UCLA for two testing sessions. In addition, we asked for permission to contact the school that their child was attending in order to arrange two observation sessions at school. Parents were paid $25 to cover their costs for each session at UCLA and teachers were paid $10 for completing a set of questionnaires about the child. The study was explained to the parents and teachers when they were contacted and, then, again at the time of the first assessment. At this time, parents and teachers completed consent forms, certified by the Institutional Review Board at UCLA. The study was explained also to children whose language ages on our assessments were above 8 years, and they were asked to sign assent forms.

Some families were willing to have their child seen at home or in an institution but did not want to bring their child to UCLA. In those cases, assessments were conducted in the home or institution and observations were made with portable video equipment. Two trips were arranged to test participants whose families had moved to Northern California, Oregon, and Washington. One subject was tested in New Orleans by experimenters who attended the SRCD meeting held in that city. In these cases, school visits could not be made. When possible, children whose families had moved away were tested during family trips back to southern California. A few families brought their children back so that they could be assessed by our team.

Eight families with children in the autism group, five families with children in the Down syndrome group, and one family with a child in the developmental delay group were located out of town and were interviewed by telephone about their children's symptomatology and adaptive skills. Questionnaires also were sent to these families and were completed in some cases.

### Number and Age of Participants in Each Group at Follow-Up

At least some information was obtained on 71% of the 219 children in the original target group. For the group with autism, 51 of the 70 children (73%) have diagnostic information and 43 (61%) have assessments. Sixteen families could not be located and three families did not wish to participate. Of the 92 children with Down syndrome, 71 (77%) have information at least about adaptive skills and 66 (72%) were assessed. Fourteen families could not be located, four families did not wish to participate, two children were deceased, and one child was seriously ill with leukemia. Of the 57 children with developmental delays, 33 (58%) have some information and 32 (56%) were assessed. Fourteen families could not be located, seven families did not wish to participate, four children have serious degenerative diseases and were not assessed, and one family was involved in a legal dispute with the school system and was not contacted by us. Overall, about one fifth of the families could not be located and 6% declined participation.

The children were seen at about 10 to 12 years of age. The mean ages of the 155 participants are shown in Table 2, presented separately for each diagnostic group. The mean years since initial testing and subject gender and ethnic background also are provided in that table. As can be seen from that table, the Down syndrome group was younger than the other two groups at intake. The autistic group was significantly older than the other two groups at follow-up. Finally, the mean time between first and follow-up visit was 8 years for the sample as a whole. The developmentally delayed children were retested after a significantly shorter interval, however, than the children in the other two groups.

TABLE 2

CHARACTERISTICS OF THE FOLLOW-UP SAMPLE

| | | Autistic Group $n = 51$ | Down Syndrome Group $n = 71$ | Developmental Delay Group $n = 33$ |
|---|---|---|---|---|
| Chronological Age at | Mean | 3–11 | 2–8* | 3–6 |
| Intake in Years–Months | SD | .94 | 1.17 | 1.00 |
| Chronological Age at | Mean | 12–10* | 10–9 | 9–11 |
| Follow-Up in Years– | SD | 3.74 | 3.58 | 2.48 |
| Months | | | | |
| | Mean | 8–11 | 8–1 | 6–5* |
| Time from First Testing | SD | 3.38 | 3.01 | 2.48 |
| Gender | Males | 86% | 56% | 73% |
| Ethnic Background | Caucasian | 65% | 61% | 67% |
| Mother's Education– | Mean | 5.57 | 5.94 | 6.07 |
| Rating Scale | SD | 1.43 | 1.55 | 1.67 |

*Significantly different from other two groups.

## Representativeness of the Follow-Up Samples

In order to determine how representative the follow-up sample is of the groups originally recruited, initial ages, genders, mental ages, DQ/IQs, and socioeconomic status were compared for the 64 participants with no follow-up information and the 155 participants in a series of analyses of variance (ANOVAs). Mothers who participated had higher levels of education than nonparticipants, $F(1, 200) = 23.84$, $p < .0001$, and this was true for all groups. In addition, the participants in the developmentally delayed group were more intelligent at intake than the nonparticipants ($Ms = 65.7$ vs. $55.3$; $F(1,55) = 4.98$, $p < .013$), but this was not true for the other groups. Other than this, the participants seem to represent the original sample quite well.

## Participation in Special Education and Different Forms of Therapy

Most developmentally disabled children in the United States receive a variety of interventions provided either by schools, private therapists, or centers for the developmentally disabled. Parents were asked to fill out a questionnaire concerning the past and current participation of their children in such programs. According to this parental report, the majority of

19

the children had been in special education programs at some point in their lives. This was especially true for the children with autism, 93% of whom had been or were currently enrolled in special education. The percentages were somewhat lower for the children with Down syndrome (82%) and developmental delay (74%). The most frequent kinds of therapy were focused on speech and language. The percentages of children who had been in speech or language therapy were 83% of the autistic group, 85% of the Down syndrome group, and 74% of the developmentally delayed group. The second most frequent form of therapy was play therapy with slightly over one third of each group enrolled at some point in this kind of intervention. About one quarter of the autistic and developmentally delayed groups had some physical therapy, whereas 44% of the children with Down syndrome were reported by their parents to have had some physical therapy. The other group difference was in therapy directed toward social behaviors and skills; 45% of the children with autism had this kind of experience as opposed to 13% of the children with Down syndrome and 13% of the children with developmental delays. Thus, all the children had been enrolled in some type of therapy with the majority of children in more than one form. It should be kept in mind that these numbers are imprecise in that the parents filled out a very simple questionnaire that covered their children's entire life experiences. Precise retrospective documentation of intervention experiences would be impossible to do over such a long period of time.

## STABILITY OF THE DIAGNOSIS OF AUTISM

One of the most important questions about autism is the extent to which individuals change over time in their symptoms and level of functioning. A difficulty in attempting to determine whether diagnosis has changed is that most diagnostic systems focus on behaviors shown by young children with autism. This focus is understandable as most children are diagnosed between 3 and 6 years of age and very little rediagnosis is done in clinical settings. The symptoms change as individuals mature, however, in that social and communicative difficulties lessen and self-stimulation and ritualistic behaviors become less predominant, at least for some children. For this reason, none of the diagnostic measures are entirely appropriate for the current diagnosis of older children.

The Autism Diagnostic Interview-Revised (ADI-R; Le Couteur et al., 1989; Lord, Rutter, & Le Couteur, 1994) assesses the child's symptomatology in three different areas and takes about 1½ hours to administer. In order to meet the criteria for diagnosis of autism, children's scores have to reach preset cutoffs in all three areas. In addition, symptomatology has to be present before 3 years of age. The parents are asked about the child's behavior at age

4–5 years or when it was most abnormal (for children younger than 4–5 years) and also about current behavior. The criteria are slightly different for the "ever" and "current" scores. Despite the fact that the instrument was designed to focus on the "ever" scores, for our purposes, the "current" scores are more important.

In order to examine diagnostic change in the sample of 51 children originally diagnosed, the ADI-R (Lord et al., 1994) was administered to their parents by Dr. Shoshana Arbelle, who was trained to reliability during a workshop administered by Dr. Catherine Lord. The ADI-R was administered in person to parents, while the child was assessed in a separate room. For the eight children with autism whose families lived out of town, the ADI-R was conducted by telephone.

The ADI-R also was administered to parents of 30 of the 33 children with developmental delays. Three families of children with developmental delays (one with Prader-Willi syndrome, one with cerebral palsy, and one with early physical problems) were not administered the interview. Whereas we intended to use the ADI-R with the parents of children with Down syndrome, we discontinued the administration of this instrument after the 20th family. The parents of children with Down syndrome seemed to find the interview disturbing, because the symptoms did not apply at all to their children and the questions were confusing to them. None of the 20 children with Down syndrome whose parents were administered the ADI-R met the criteria for diagnosis based either on their past or present symptoms.

All the children originally diagnosed as autistic also were diagnosed as autistic on the ADI-R using the "ever" criterion, except for one boy who missed one criterion by 1 point. This boy had been included in the autistic group at intake since he met the criterion on two of the three diagnostic indicators, clinician's diagnosis, and observer's score on the CARS, although he did not meet the criterion for diagnosis on the ABC filled out originally during an interview with the mother. In fact, at intake, all the clinicians who interacted with this child felt that his behaviors met the criteria for diagnosis of autism. His mother's accuracy as a observer was called into question because he was seen to demonstrate behaviors in his mother's presence that the mother did not report. At follow-up, this boy did not make the "current" criterion for autism on the ADI-R administered to the mother. This case illustrates one problem in relying on a sole informant for diagnostic information, as we have done at follow-up.

The vast majority of the children originally diagnosed with autism continued to show severe enough symptoms to meet the criteria for current diagnosis at follow-up. Only five children (excluding the boy discussed above) showed a diminution in symptomatology great enough so that their "current" scores no longer reached all the criteria for diagnosis. One child missed one criterion by 1 point. Of the three children who met only one

21

criterion, one boy continued to be moderately mentally retarded with an IQ of 38 and two boys were in the borderline range with IQs of 79 and 83. The child who did not meet any of the criteria was of normal intelligence with an IQ of 102 although his language was about 2 years delayed. Thus, at follow-up, none of the children were completely symptom free. Forty-five of the fifty children continued to meet the full diagnostic criteria for autism.

Only 4 of the 30 developmentally delayed children who were administered the ADI-R met the "current" criteria for diagnosis. These four children met the "ever" criteria as well although their intake information did not support these retrospective accounts. Three of the four had been scored on the CARS at intake and their scores did not exceed the cutoff for diagnosis. In two cases, the parents were interviewed with the ABC at intake and these scores did not meet criteria for diagnosis. One subject was a 17-year-old boy who had been hospitalized at the Neuropsychiatric Institute at age 4 years and then placed in a residential institution that was at considerable distance from his family, where he has remained for the subsequent years, so that the reliability of his mother's retrospective report may be questionable. In our clinical judgment, only one of these four children is currently autistic and, perhaps, should have been diagnosed originally with autism. His data have been kept in the developmentally delayed group because he did not meet clinical criteria for autism when seen initially. With the possible exception of this boy, no child was diagnosed as autistic who did not originally have the diagnosis and most remain delayed in language and/or mental development but without autistic symptomatology by all accounts.

## STABILITY OF THE DIAGNOSIS OF MENTAL RETARDATION

The IQ cutoff for the diagnosis of mental retardation is 70; children with IQs of 70 and over are not considered to be mentally retarded. One question of interest is the extent to which children with autism and Down syndrome retain IQs that are low enough for them to be considered mentally retarded. This issue can be addressed in this study because of the repeated testing of intelligence, albeit with different instruments at different ages.

The method of assessing intelligence was altered at follow-up because of the availability of the revised Stanford-Binet (Thorndike, Hagen, & Sattler, 1986). Despite our reluctance to alter measurement techniques and, thereby, add measurement variance to our comparisons, the use of increasingly out-of-date assessments did not seem justifiable. All participants who were able to receive basal scores on the vocabulary subtest of the Stanford-Binet were tested with that measure. Children who did not have sufficient vocabulary knowledge to receive basal scores on the Stanford-Binet were tested with the Bayley Scales.

Four Stanford-Binet subtests, Vocabulary, Bead Memory, Pattern Analysis, and Quantitative Analysis, were administered, which allowed the calculation of a mean mental age on the four subtests and an overall IQ. These four subtests were used because the manual recommends their inclusion in short forms of the Stanford-Binet. The Bayley Scales, like the previously administered Cattell Scales, furnish a mental age for each subject. Ratio Developmental Quotients were calculated by dividing mental age by chronological age as had been done previously with the Cattell Scales. This was necessary with the Bayley Scales because the chronological ages of the participants far exceeds the ages of the standardization sample. The majority of children were administered the Stanford-Binet, 105 of the 141 who were tested. Thirty-six children were administered the Bayley Scales, 18 children in the autistic group, 11 children in the Down syndrome group, and 7 children in the developmentally delayed group.

During the period that assessments were administered, the new version of the Bayley Scales was published so we changed instruments. Given the timing of the testing, this resulted in the children with autism being tested with the original Bayley Scales, whereas most of the children with Down syndrome and developmental delays were tested with the revised Bayley Scales. Scores on the revised Bayley Scales tend to be lower than those on the original Bayley Scales (see, for example, Goldstein, Fogle, Weber, & O'Shea, 1995). For this reason, the Bayley mental scores for the children with autism may have been inflated by the use of the original Bayley Scales although these scores were lower than those for the other mentally retarded, nonautistic children ($Ms = 19.2$ for the autistic group and 26.3 for the mentally retarded group). Because of the possibility of test effects, language age rather than mental age is used as the principal measure for matching the groups in this study.

In order to determine the extent to which children remained mentally retarded, the diagnostic groups were subdivided by the IQ cutoff of 70 at both the initial and follow-up testings. The number of children in each subgroup is shown in Table 3. As can be seen from the table, 11 children with autism who originally tested in the mentally retarded range moved out of that range at follow-up whereas one child declined enough in IQ to be considered mentally retarded only at follow-up. Although only 9% of the autistic group was not mentally retarded at the 3 to 5-year age period, a full 33% were not retarded at follow-up. One of the questions to be addressed later in this monograph is whether early characteristics can be identified that differentiate the 11 children who show a rise in IQ from the 28 children who do not.

TABLE 3

NUMBER OF CHILDREN WITH MENTAL RETARDATION

| Intake | Autistic Group Follow-Up | | | Down Syndrome Group Follow-Up | | | Developmental Delayed Group Follow-Up | | |
|---|---|---|---|---|---|---|---|---|---|
| | IQ < 70 | IQ ≥ 70 | Total N | IQ < 70 | IQ ≥ 70 | Total N | IQ < 70 | IQ ≥ 70 | Total N |
| IQ < 70 | 28 | 11 | 39 | 40 | 0 | 40 | 14 | 4 | 18 |
| IQ ≥ 70 | 1 | 3 | 4 | 26 | 0 | 26 | 5 | 9 | 14 |
| | 29 | 14 | 43 | 66 | 0 | 66 | 19 | 13 | 32 |

The children with Down syndrome show a very different pattern from both of the other groups. Fully 40% of the group did not test in the mentally retarded range initially. No child in the group, however, has an IQ higher than 70 by the mid-school years.

The pattern of change in the developmentally delayed group is more like that of the children with autism than the children with Down syndrome. In both the autistic and delayed groups, about one fourth of the children change in terms of the diagnosis of mental retardation. For the delayed children, however, the percentage who change in both directions is close, whereas the children with autism predominantly move out of the classification of mental retardation.

One explanation for the decline in intelligence in children with Down syndrome is that intelligence tests may be less reliable with them than with other groups. This explanation has been suggested by Jennifer Wishart, who has evidence that children with Down syndrome often do not show their best skills during testing (Wishart & Duffy, 1990). In her study, children with Down syndrome were administered the Bayley Scales twice over a 1-to-2 week interval at each age. Stability of passing items was less for the children with Down syndrome than would be predicted from the standard error of measurement provided in the Bayley manual for the normal standardization sample. The stability of performance of the children with Down syndrome could not be compared with the stability of performance of normal children or children with other developmental delays as there were no control groups in this study. For this reason, the conclusion that reliability of developmental assessments is less for children with Down syndrome than other children is still open to question. The observation that children with Down syndrome are not very motivated to solve tasks such as those on the Bayley mental scale, however, is in line with other results (Ruskin, Kasari, Mundy, & Sigman, 1994; Ruskin, Mundy, Kasari, & Sigman, 1994).

In order to evaluate whether the developmental assessment was less reliable for the children with Down syndrome in this study, the correlations between the original DQs and the 1-year follow-up DQs were compared for those children who had both tests. The test-retest reliability over the course of the year was roughly comparable for the four groups with the Down syndrome group showing the highest stability. The correlations for the four groups were as follows: $r(21) = .62, p < .002$, for the autistic children; $r(42) = .76, p < .0000$, for the children with Down syndrome; $r(28) = .66, p < .0001$, for the children with developmental delays; and $r(21) = .75, p < .0000$, for the typically developing children. Therefore, the decline in intelligence in the Down syndrome sample did not seem to result from some short-term lack of stability in their testing performance.

## LONG-TERM STABILITY IN INTELLIGENCE QUOTIENTS AND MENTAL AGES

Another way to examine long-term group stability and change in intelligence is to examine mean DQ/IQs and mental ages over time. Initial scores were compared with follow-up scores for the children in each group. Whereas all the children show significant gains in mental age, only the children with Down syndrome show a significant decline in intelligence, $t(65) = 10.50, p < .0001$ (see Table 4).

TABLE 4

Intelligence Scores and Mental Ages at Intake and Follow-Up

|  |  | Autistic Group $n = 43$ | Down Syndrome Group $n = 66$ | Developmental Delay Group $n = 32$ |
|---|---|---|---|---|
| Initial DQ/IQ | Mean | 51.3 | 66.05* | 65.5 |
|  | SD | 13.6 | 17.1 | 17.3 |
|  | Range | 34–89 | 36–107 | 36–101 |
| Follow-Up DQ/IQ | Mean | 48.5 | 45.8 | 63.1 |
|  | SD | 31.5 | 11.2 | 29.4 |
|  | Range | 12–116 | 18–65 | 18–128 |
| Initial MA | Mean | 25.4* | 20.7* | 28.7* |
|  | SD | 11.4 | 8.1 | 11.7 |
|  | Range | 14–76 | 9–46 | 10–56 |
| Follow-Up MA | Mean | 60.9 | 49.4 | 68.0 |
|  | SD | 44.1 | 13.9 | 31.5 |
|  | Range | 13–182 | 20–89 | 20–142 |

*Significantly different between intake and follow-up, $p < .05$.

The change in intelligence was compared for the three groups with an ANOVA, partialling out initial intelligence and initial age. The covariation of initial age was necessary because the groups varied in initial ages and initial age was negatively related to DQ/IQ in the sample of children with Down syndrome, $r(64) = -.61, p < .0001$. Follow-up age did not have to be used as a covariate, because there was no association between follow-up age and intelligence for any group. The decline in intelligence for the Down syndrome group was significantly greater than for the developmentally delayed group but not than the autistic group when initial age was considered.

In order to determine if the more marked decline in intelligence among groups was due to the fact that the children with Down syndrome were younger when they were tested initially than the children in the other groups, comparisons were made of intelligence at all three time periods for each group. The mean IQs of the children with autism and the children with developmental delays were almost identical across time periods. In contrast, the IQs of the children with Down syndrome were significantly different at all age periods. For those children with Down syndrome who were administered intelligence tests at all age periods, mean IQs declined from 70.8 at the first testing to 62.3 at the second testing and 45.7 at the third testing. This is a drop of 6.5 points over the course of the 1st year and a further 16.6 over the longer time course. As a comparison, the mean IQs of the developmentally delayed children tested at the first and third sessions (when their mean ages were within 1 month of those of the children with Down syndrome tested at the second and third sessions) were 67.9 and 68.1 respectively. Thus, the greater decline of the IQ of the children with Down syndrome is not only due to their younger age at initial testing.

There is also a difference among groups in terms of individual development. The standard deviation is close to the 15 points expected on these kinds of tests at initial assessment of all three groups (see Table 4). The standard deviation more than doubles at follow-up for the autistic group, however, and increases for the developmentally delayed group, whereas it declines for the Down syndrome group.

## CONTINUITY IN INTELLIGENCE OVER TIME

To assess the extent of individual continuity in intelligence, Pearson product moment correlations were calculated between the initial DQ/IQs and follow-up DQ/IQs for the children in each diagnostic group. The results showed that initial DQ/IQs predict later DQ/IQs for children in every group, $r(40) = .44, p < .004$, for the autistic group; $r(63) = .41, p < .006$, for the Down syndrome group, and $r(29) = .71, p < .0001$, for the developmentally delayed group. These correlations are presented with age at intake covaried although the correlations are virtually the same when initial age is ignored. Thus, even though there is movement between mentally retarded and nonretarded groups, initial level of intelligence does predict between 16 and 50% of the variance in intelligence during the school years.

In terms of individual change, about half the children with autism (22 of 43) and developmental delays (14 of 32) showed increases in intelligence test scores, whereas only 6 of the 66 children with Down syndrome had higher scores at follow-up than at intake. For the six children with Down syndrome whose scores were higher, the increase was only 4.17 points in contrast to 22.38 points for the children with autism and 17.21 points for the children with developmental delays. There were no group differences in the amount of decline for those children whose intelligence scores were lower; the mean drop across diagnostic groups was 23 points.


## DISCUSSION

In summary, the diagnosis of autism remained stable over time. The vast majority of children continued to be severely affected so that they met criteria for the diagnosis when current symptomatology was considered. Even the few children whose symptomatology by parents' report diminished enough so that they no longer met all the criteria for diagnosis continued to have severe cognitive and language problems. This group of children has been involved in many different intervention and education programs over the years. Despite their participation in intervention programs of various kinds, the children continued to be diagnosed with autism. Participation in more effective interventions, however, may diminish this stability.

It is possible that some children who are less severely affected early in life may have a more variable course. In this study, children were classified as autistic only if they were universally considered to be so by large groups of clinicians who were very familiar with them or if they satisfied diagnostic criteria from two different sources. Children with milder symptomatology who were considered autistic by some clinicians and not others or met the criteria for autism only by clinicians' report and not that of the parents or an outside observer were not included in the sample of autistic children. A group of children with less certain diagnosis might show less stability over time.

In contrast to their diagnoses, a proportion of the sample of children with autism showed remarkable intellectual growth. A full one third of the mentally retarded, autistic children developed sufficient intellectual skills to no longer be considered mentally retarded although they remained autistic. We know that nonretarded autistic individuals (often referred to as high-functioning) have more life options than retarded autistic individuals. In Chapter VI, we will show that social involvement in the school playground increases as a function of cognitive and language abilities in children with autism. Thus, this advancement in intelligence is extremely important in terms of the child's life course even if it does not cure the problems associated with the child's autism. For this reason, in Chapter III, we will try to identify some of the early characteristics that distinguish the children who remain mentally retarded from those who do not.

As a group, the children with Down syndrome showed a very different course of intellectual development. A large proportion of the sample started out with intelligence test scores above the mentally retarded range but every child with Down syndrome scored in the mentally retarded range at follow-up. As discussed earlier, this change has been documented previously in the research literature. Four explanations for the decline can be suggested. First, as discussed above, intelligence tests may be less reliable with children with Down syndrome. Second, the decline may be partly a function of the type of skills considered to be part of intelligence at different ages. In infancy and the early toddler years, children do not understand or use language, so intelligence is measured in terms of nonverbal skills that are adaptive during these age periods. By 3 years of age, however, language develops and becomes very critical for adaptation so that intelligence tests used for children older than 3 years tap many more verbal skills than developmental assessments of younger children. Part of the reason for the decline in intelligence in children with Down syndrome may be because their specific problems with language are not manifested until they reach the age where language is required both in intelligence tests as well as in their lives. Another possible explanation is that the children are actually losing ability along with some progressive brain dysfunctions. Finally, intensive intervention programs taper off after the preschool years so that the children have much less help in gaining new skills and maintaining those acquired earlier. These explanations cannot be tested in this study.

At follow-up, the group of children with Down syndrome is much more homogenous than the other two groups. Despite this, all the groups show stability in intelligence over time in that children who are more intelligent at the first testing continue to be so 8 years later. For example, the children with autism who are no longer mentally retarded at follow-up were generally the more intelligent children in the group at intake. At the same time, the amount of variance accounted for in outcome IQ by initial IQ is 17–19% in the autistic and Down syndrome groups, which means that other factors contribute to the change in intelligence over time. In the next chapter, we will examine children's communicative and symbolic skills that contribute to their social and intellectual growth.

# III. NONVERBAL COMMUNICATION, PLAY, AND LANGUAGE SKILLS

Communication skills are the most important prerequisites for social interaction. Individuals who cannot talk are limited in their social relationships in that only very primitive concepts can be communicated nonverbally. On the other hand, nonverbal communication skills are extremely important in the early life of the child. Nonverbal skills may reflect the child's motivation to communicate as well as some understanding of how to communicate that may be necessary, along with representational skills, for the acquisition of language. For this reason, much of our research has been devoted to identifying strengths and weaknesses in the nonverbal and verbal communication skills of children with autism and Down syndrome.

As mentioned in Chapter I, our earlier research has shown a specific deficit in joint attention in young children with autism. Young children with autism were much less likely to initiate joint attention or respond to bids for joint attention than samples of normal children of the same mental and language age and samples of developmentally delayed children, including both children with Down syndrome and other forms of mental retardation. Moreover, joint attention skills were associated with language abilities both concurrently and 1 year later in children with autism.

There was also some evidence in our research that children with Down syndrome were less likely to request objects or assistance with objects than normal children of the same developmental level. This deficit was not as striking as the deficit in joint attention in children with autism in a number of ways. First, the children with Down syndrome showed a reduction in the frequency of requesting, not an absence of requesting, so that most children with Down syndrome did make some requests for objects or assistance with objects. In contrast, many children with autism did not initiate joint attention or follow the gaze of others at all. Second, the joint attention deficit was clearly unique to autism as it was not shown by heterogeneous groups of children with developmental delays. On the other hand, the uniqueness of the requesting deficit to the Down syndrome group is unknown. The only comparison of the nonverbal communicative behaviors of a small group of children with other forms of delay and those of the children with Down syndrome showed no differences in the frequency of requesting between the groups.

## COMMUNICATION, PLAY, AND LANGUAGE SKILLS AT INITIAL ASSESSMENT

The first aim of this chapter is to reexamine these findings using the entire sample of children whose nonverbal and verbal skills have been examined. Given the small samples in previous studies, we have used a strategy of replicating findings from one study to the next. In this monograph, nonverbal and verbal skills and the concurrent associations between them will be compared for the three groups of developmentally disordered children as well as the group of typical children who were initially studied but not followed over time. This monograph provides the first opportunity to reexamine the previous findings with a large sample of children in each diagnostic group so that the uniqueness of deficits can be examined more precisely than was previously possible.

### Group Differences in Nonverbal Communication Skills

Nonverbal communication skills were measured in a standardized social interaction between the experimenter and the child. In this procedure, the child and a tester sit facing each other at a small table. A set of toys are in view but out of reach of the child. The tester presents a variety of toys and plays a series of games aimed at eliciting turn taking. In addition, on several trials, the tester points to the left, right, and behind the child while emphatically saying the child's name. This procedure, called the Early Social Communication Scales (ESCS) by its designers, has been described in detail in two manuals (Mundy, Hogan, & Doehring, 1996; Seibert, Hogan, & Mundy, 1982).

The procedure is videotaped to record the full-face and upper body view of the child. Frequencies of behavior are recorded by trained observers. Observations are grouped into three mutually exclusive categories: requesting, joint attention, and social interaction. Each of these categories is composed of a variable number of behaviors. The requesting category includes behaviors used to direct attention to objects or events in order to request aid in obtaining the object or repetition of an event. The joint attention category also involves the coordination of the child's and tester's attention to objects or events. The instrumental function of these behaviors is less apparent, however, because the object is within reach or the event is ongoing. The social interaction behaviors involve eliciting attention or physical contact from the tester and engaging in turn-taking with objects. A separate index of the child's capacities to respond appropriately is also scored. The measure of responsiveness to joint attention is scored dichotomously over six trials according to whether or not a child turns his or her head and eyes in the correct direction. Interrater reliability has been established on this scale multiple times and mean generalizability coefficients are at about .80.

Coding of behavioral data was carried out by observers who did not know the hypotheses of the studies. Although coders were usually aware of the group membership of the children with Down syndrome and normal children, the diagnoses of the children with autism and developmental delays were not obvious. Moreover, the use of microanalytic coding techniques made it less likely for observer bias to influence the coding.

All group comparisons of data throughout this study were carried out in four stages. First, for any comparison, the mean language ages of the samples for whom data were available were compared in an ANOVA. If the groups were different ($p < .101$), then the data from the children with the highest language scores were deleted from the comparisons. In practice, this meant deleting data from the sample of children with developmental delays as their language ages tended to be higher than the other groups at both testing points. For most of the comparisons of the intake data, data from 8 to 10 children with developmental delays were deleted, whereas, for the comparison of the follow-up data, data from 4 children with developmental delays were deleted.

In the second stage, data were compared across groups with a multivariate analysis of variance (MANOVA) for all variables where dependent variables were significantly intercorrelated. In those cases where the MANOVA was significant, follow-up ANOVAs were calculated to identify the particular dependent variables accounting for the group differences. Finally, for those dependent variables that showed group differences, significant differences between groups were identified using Newman-Keuls post hoc comparisons.

In order to determine whether there were group differences in communicative skills, the extent to which children initiated joint attention, requesting, and social interactions or responded to bids for joint attention and social interaction were compared across groups in a MANOVA. The data from the 10 developmentally delayed children and the 4 typically developing children with the highest language ages was dropped from the analyses so that the mean language ages of the four groups were equivalent, $p > .17$. The group effect in the MANOVA of the nonverbal communication data was significant according to Wilk's criterion, $\lambda = .69$, $F(15, 712.6) = 6.87$, $p < .0001$, so that separate ANOVAs were calculated for each variable. These results strongly replicated the previous findings of group differences in initiating joint attention, $F(3, 262) = 20.02$, $p < .00001$, and responding to bids for joint attention, $F(3, 262) = 10.23$, $p < .00001$. Autistic children initiated joint attention much less than the children in the other groups, autistic group less than other groups, all $ps < .0001$.

The children with autism also responded to bids for joint attention less than the children in the other groups; autistic group less than Down syndrome group, $p < .002$, autistic group less than developmentally delayed and typically developing children, $ps < .0001$, according to the Newman-Keuls test. The other groups of developmentally disabled children showed no differences from each other or from the typically developing children in the frequency of initiating or the percentage of responding to bids for joint attention (see figures 1 and 2).

Although the results also replicated the previous findings that children with Down syndrome request objects and assistance less than typically developing children, the current analyses demonstrated that this deficit is not unique to children with Down syndrome (see figure 3). The typically developing children attempted to regulate the behavior of the experimenter more than the children in all three developmentally disabled groups, $F(3, 262) = 11.22$, $p < .00001$. The differences were significant for all comparisons according to the Newman-Keuls test; autistic group less than typically developing group, $p < .0001$, Down syndrome group less than typically developing group, $p < .002$, developmentally delayed group less than typically developing group, $p < .03$. According to the Newman-Keuls test, the children with autism engaged in behavior regulation significantly less than the

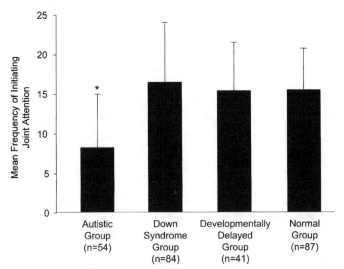

FIGURE 1.—Mean frequencies and standard deviations of initiating joint attention on the Early Social Communication Scale by the children with autism, Down syndrome, developmental delays, and the typically developing children. *Indicates that the children with autism initiated joint attention significantly less than the other groups of children.

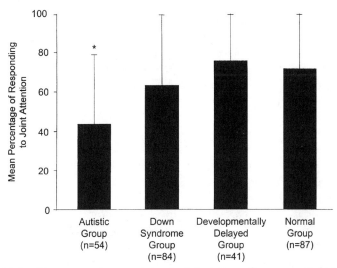

FIGURE 2.—Mean percentages and standard deviations of responses to bids for joint attention on the Early Social Communication Scale by the children with autism, Down syndrome, developmental delays, and the typically developing children. *Indicates that the children with autism responded to bids for joint attention significantly less than the other groups of children.

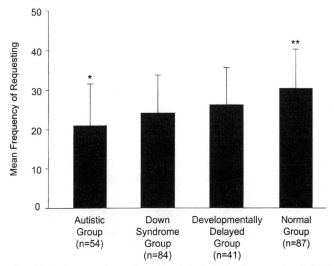

FIGURE 3.—Mean frequencies and standard deviations of requesting behaviors on the Early Social Communication Scale by the children with autism, Down syndrome, developmental delays, and the typically developing children. *Indicates that the children with autism requested objects or assistance significantly less than the children with developmental delays and the typically developing children. **Indicates that typically developing children requested objects or assistance significantly more than all the other groups.

children in the developmentally delayed group, $p < .02$, but not than the Down syndrome group. The frequency of requesting behaviors was similar for the children with Down syndrome and the other two groups of developmentally disabled children. If the deficit in requesting was unique to children with Down syndrome, they would have been expected to differ from the other two groups in terms of their frequency of requesting behaviors.

The groups of children did not differ very much in the frequency with which they initiated or responded to bids for dyadic social interactions. The children with autism initiated social bids less than the children with Down syndrome, $p < .03$, according to the Newman-Keuls test, but there were no other group differences (see figures 4 and 5).

The results demonstrate that children with autism have a specific and unique deficit in joint attention. On the other hand, the children with Down syndrome do not differ in nonverbal communication from children with other developmental disorders. They only differ from the typically developing children in the extent to which they attempt to regulate the behavior of others. Their nonverbal communication skills are superior to those of the children with autism in almost all regards and equivalent to those of the developmentally delayed children. Whereas they do show a deficit in requesting behaviors in contrast to typically developing children, this deficit is shared by all the developmentally disabled children.

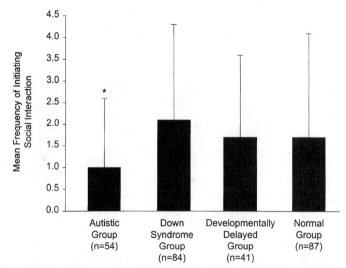

FIGURE 4.—Mean frequencies and standard deviations of initiating social interactions on the Early Social Communication Scale by the children with autism, Down syndrome, developmental delays, and the typically developing children. *Indicates that the children with autism initiated social interaction significantly less than the children with Down syndrome.

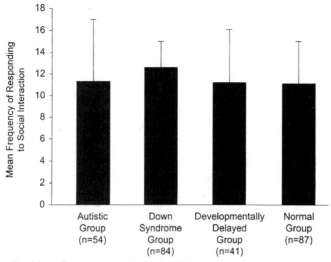

FIGURE 5.—Mean frequencies and standard deviations of responding to bids for social interaction on the Early Social Communication Scale by the children with autism, Down syndrome, developmental delays, and the typically developing children.

## Concurrent Associations Between Nonverbal Communication and Language Abilities

Both theory and empirical evidence suggest that nonverbal communication skills are prerequisites for language development. Our previous evidence had shown that concurrent level of language skills was associated with joint attention in children with autism and with behavior regulation in children with Down syndrome. In order to assess these concurrent relations with larger samples, correlations were computed between the nonverbal communication skills and measured language abilities.

The choice of measures of language level has been of concern throughout this research project. As the children in the sample vary greatly in language abilities, a language assessment is required that covers a broad variations of skills. In addition, the examination of both language comprehension and use is important. Linguists often prefer measures of language production such as mean length of utterance. Many of the children in these samples, however, do not speak spontaneously very often so such an assessment would require frequent, lengthy observations and, even then, might underestimate the children's capacities.

At the start of this research program, we were unable to identify a standardized language assessment. For this reason, the children's receptive and expressive language-age equivalents were determined by a clinical linguist who assessed the children over several sessions. These clinical assessments

35

seemed valid based on two pieces of evidence. First, language age as determined by the linguist was highly correlated ($r = .73$) with language age as reported by parents for a sample of 18 children whose parents were asked to complete the Receptive and Expressive Emergent Language Scale (REEL; Bzoch & League, 1971). In addition, the linguist's receptive language ages were highly correlated with a laboratory measure of language comprehension, $r(42) = .76$ (Beckwith & Thompson, 1976).

In all subsequent studies, language abilities were assessed with the Reynell Scales of Language Abilities (Reynell, 1977). These scales are particularly useful because they cover a wide range of language skills—from age 12 months to 7 years. In addition, age equivalent scores can be calculated for both receptive and expressive language abilities. For our purposes, a mean age equivalent across both domains was calculated in addition to the separate receptive and expressive age scores.

Correlations between the three measures of language age and the frequency of nonverbal communicative behaviors were calculated for a sample of children whose nonverbal communication skills had been compared. The findings were similar for receptive, expressive, and overall language age so only the latter are presented (see Table 5). The results showed that language ages were associated concurrently with the percentage of responses to bids for joint attention for all the children and with the frequency of initiation of joint attention for all the children except the typically developing children. (Frequency of initiating joint attention was significantly correlated with language age for the typically developing children if data from the whole sample of 91 children were used.) In addition, the percentage of time that the autistic children responded to bids for social interaction and the frequency of behavior regulation gestures made by the children with Down syndrome were correlated with language ages. This last correlation was very low and

TABLE 5

CORRELATIONS BETWEEN COMMUNICATIVE ACTS AND CONCURRENT LANGUAGE SKILLS

|  | Autistic Group $n = 54$ | DS Group $n = 84$ | DD Group $n = 41$ | Normal Group $n = 87$ |
|---|---|---|---|---|
| Initiates Joint Attention | .51*** | .46*** | .44** | .10 |
| Initiates Behavior Regulation | .18 | .22* | .25 | .09 |
| Initiates Social Interaction | .17 | .20 | −.08 | −.09 |
| Responds to Joint Attention | .72*** | .41*** | .48** | .43*** |
| Responds to Social Interaction | .43* | .07 | .04 | −.05 |

*$p < .05$
**$p < .01$
***$p < .001$

TABLE 6

CORRELATIONS BETWEEN COMMUNICATION ACTS AND
SHORT-TERM GAINS IN EXPRESSIVE LANGUAGE SKILLS

|  | Autistic Group $n = 41$ | DS Group $n = 56$ | DD Group $n = 28$ |
|---|---|---|---|
| Initiates Joint Attention[a] | .33* | .40** | −.33 |
| Initiates Behavior Regulation | .36* | .25 | −.01 |
| Initiates Social Interaction | .21 | .52*** | .01 |
| Responds to Joint Attention | .44** | .19 | .12 |
| Responds to Social Interaction | .34* | −.15 | −.53** |

[a]Correlations with intake expressive language and chronological ages covaried.
*$p < .05$
**$p < .01$
***$p < .001$

was significant partly because of the large size of the Down syndrome sample, although the associations for the children with Down syndrome are similar to those reported by Smith & von Tetzchner (1986).

Most of the samples in this study were retested 1 year after their original testing. As the Reynell Scales were readministered both times, it was possible to determine whether nonverbal communication measures were predictors of language gain from one year to the next by calculating the correlations between the nonverbal communication scores and the follow-up language ages with intake chronological and language ages covaried. There were significant predictions of both overall language age and expressive language age, but not receptive language age, for the children in both the autistic and Down syndrome groups. The predictions of nonverbal communication behaviors to expressive language abilities are shown in Table 6. The frequencies of all the nonverbal communication behaviors, except initiates social interaction, were predictive of expressive language gains for the children with autism. For the children with Down syndrome, the frequencies of initiation of joint attention and social interaction were predictive of expressive language gains. Thus, not only were nonverbal communicative skills concurrently associated with language abilities, but autistic and Down syndrome children with more advanced nonverbal communicative skills also gained more over the course of 1 year than was true for children with less advanced nonverbal communicative skills.

## Representational Play Skills

In addition to nonverbal communication skills, play skills of almost all the participants were observed. Representational play skills are important

37

TABLE 7

CODED CATEGORIES OF PLAY BEHAVIORS

**Functional play.** Four different types of functional acts were recorded:

1.  Object-directed (e.g., Placing the top on the teapot or pushing the truck into the garage)
2.  Self-directed (e.g., Brushing one's hair)
3.  Doll-directed (e.g., Feeding a doll with a spoon)
4.  Other-directed (e.g., Holding the telephone receiver to the mother's ear)

**Symbolic play.** Three types of symbolic acts were recorded:

1.  Substitution play—the use of an object as if it were another object (e.g., Using a teacup as if it were a telephone receiver)
2.  Agent play—the use of a doll as an independent agent of action (e.g., Propping a bottle in the doll's arms as if it could feed itself)
3.  Imaginary play—creation of objects or people having no physical representation in the immediate environment (e.g., Making pouring sounds as imaginary tea is poured from a teapot into a cup)

The number of different instances of each category of play is recorded.

for children's development in many ways. First, children demonstrate their level of understanding about objects and other people during play in ways that they are unable to do in language. Many theorists consider that children have to achieve certain levels of symbolic understanding in order to develop language skills. For this reason, the kinds of play children engage in can be used to index their nonverbal representational system. Second, play is the context for peer interaction in the lives of children through much of the school years. Thus, children who cannot play alone may not be able to engage in social activities with their peers because they do not have sufficient symbolic play skills.

The play skills of the children were assessed in a structured setting in which the experimenter presented the child with groups of related toys, such as a doll, a doll's hairbrush, and a doll's mirror. A second experimenter observed and recorded the child's spontaneous play on a checklist. Play behaviors were grouped into functional acts and symbolic acts (see Table 7 for descriptions). Reliability on observations of these behaviors has been established several times on different samples and mean generalizability coefficients tend to be around .85.

## Group Differences in Representational Play Skills

In order to determine whether there were group differences in representational play skills, the number of different functional and symbolic play acts used by the children were compared across groups. Initial mental and language ages were entered into the MANOVA and each ANOVA as a covariate because the groups could not be equalized on language ages as had been possible for the samples tested on nonverbal communication skills. The overall MANOVA was significant using the Wilk's criterion, $\lambda =$ .84, $F(6, 482) = 6.95$, $p < .0001$. There were significant group differences in both forms of play, $F(2,172) = 15.39$, $p < .0001$, for number of different functional play acts, and $F(2,172) = 15.99$, $p < .0001$, for number of different symbolic play acts. The children with Down syndrome showed more representational play of both kinds than all three other groups, including the typically developing children (see figures 6 and 7). The autistic children engaged in a smaller number of functional play acts than the children with Down syndrome, $p < .0001$, but not than the children with developmental delays or the typically developing children. The children with autism engaged in a smaller number of different symbolic acts than any of the other groups, autistic group less than Down syndrome, typically developing and developmentally delayed groups, $p$s < .001, .001, .02, respectively.

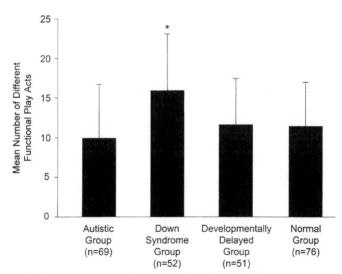

FIGURE 6.—Mean number and standard deviation of different functional play acts during a structured play situation administered to children with autism, Down syndrome, developmental delays, and the typically developing children. *Indicates that the children with Down syndrome used significantly more play acts of different kinds than the other groups of children.

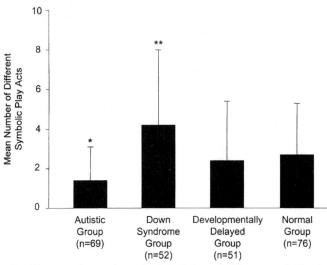

FIGURE 7.—Mean number and standard deviation of different symbolic play acts during a structured play situation administered to children with autism, Down syndrome, developmental delays, and the typically developing children. * Indicates that the children with autism used significantly fewer symbolic play acts of different kinds than all the other groups. ** Indicates that the children with Down syndrome used significantly more symbolic play acts of different kinds than all other groups.

## Concurrent Associations Between Representational Play Skills and Language Abilities

To evaluate the associations between play and language skills, correlations were calculated between these skills (see Table 8). Language skills were significantly correlated with both play variables for all groups.

The prediction of 1-year gains in language skills from representational play behaviors was assessed in the same manner as has been reported for

TABLE 8

Correlations Between Play Behaviors and Concurrent Language Skills

| Number of Play Acts | Autistic Group $n = 69$ | DS Group $n = 52$ | DD Group $n = 51$ | Normal Group $n = 76$ |
|---|---|---|---|---|
| Functional Play | .34*[a] | .39** | .56***[a] | .24* |
| Symbolic Play | .60***[a] | .44*** | .43**[a] | .23* |

[a]Remains significant when mental age covaried.
*$p < .05$
**$p < .01$
***$p < .001$

nonverbal communication skills. Representational play skills predicted 1-year language gains for the developmentally delayed children in that the number of different functional and symbolic play acts predicted to language age 1 year later when initial chronological and language ages were covaried, $rs$ (29) = .36 and .51, respectively. Representational play skills did not predict language gains for the children with autism and Down syndrome. The reason for the differential prediction between children with autism and children with developmental delays is not clear as language skills were equally stable over 1 year for both groups.

## Concurrent Associations Between Nonverbal Communication and Play Skills

Children who are more advanced in their nonverbal communication and social skills might also be expected to be more advanced in their representational understanding. Children's play almost always symbolizes social occurrences so that the paucity of symbolic engagement might result from a lack of understanding of other people and their experiences. Conversely, representational understanding must play some part in knowledge of others. In order to assess the extent to which these domains are related, correlations were computed between the frequency with which the children initiated joint attention and the percentage of response to bids for joint attention with the number of different functional and symbolic acts shown during play. As can be seen in Table 9, all the correlations were significant for the children with autism. For the other children, the number of different functional play acts was correlated only with the percentage of responding to bids for joint attention. The number of different symbolic play acts was correlated with percentage of responding to bids for joint attention only for the children with Down syndrome. When mental age was covaried, the associations between play behaviors and response to joint attention were no longer significant for any group.

Given that play and nonverbal communication skills were significantly intercorrelated and both were associated with language age, the question arises whether one domain is particularly responsible for the associations with language. A series of hierarchical regressions was calculated in which the two joint attention variables were entered as a block and the two play variables (number of different functional and symbolic acts) were entered as a block with language age as the dependent measure. The pattern of results differed across samples. For the children with autism and developmental delays, both nonverbal communication and play contributed significantly to the hierarchical regression, no matter what order these were entered. The four variables together accounted for 62% and 60% of the variance in language scores. For the Down syndrome group, either block of variables entered into

TABLE 9

CORRELATIONS BETWEEN COMMUNICATIVE AND PLAY BEHAVIORS

| Joint Attention | Autistic Group $n = 54$ | | DS Group $n = 43$ | | DD Group $n = 37$ | | Normal Group $n = 61$ | |
|---|---|---|---|---|---|---|---|---|
| | Functional | Symbolic | Functional | Symbolic | Functional | Symbolic | Functional | Symbolic |
| Initiates | .49***[a] | .54****[a] | .30 | .09 | .09 | -.06 | .13 | .10 |
| Responds | .32* | .43** | .43** | .43** | .49** | .27 | .29* | .14* |

[a]Remains significant when mental age is covaried.
*p < .05
** p < .01
***p < .001

the regression, depending which was entered first, and the two variables accounted for 23% of the variance for either block. Only the nonverbal communication variables were responsible for associations with language for the normal sample and accounted for 16% of the variance. Thus, language acquisition seemed most tied to joint attention and play skills for the autistic and developmentally delayed children.

## COMMUNICATION AND LANGUAGE SKILLS AT FOLLOW-UP

### Continuity of Nonverbal Communication Deficits and Skills

One purpose of the follow-up study was to determine whether the deficits identified in the early years of the children's lives continued to exist as they grew up. Given the limitations in nonverbal communication shown by the children with autism, we wished to ascertain whether the autistic group continued to initiate and respond to bids for joint attention less than the other groups later in life. In order to examine their nonverbal communication skills, the Early Social Communication Scale (ESCS) was slightly modified so that the activities and toys were more appropriate for older children. This was done because, in our pilot work for the follow-up study, we came to realize that some of the materials we had used when the children were younger seemed infantile to some of the participants tested at older ages. Moreover, parents and caregivers who were encouraging their children to maintain more mature behavior patterns were often uncomfortable with toys designed for infants.

As in the previous version, the child was seated at a table across from the experimenter and a set of toys was placed on a tray to the left of the experimenter and out of the child's reach. Several toys were presented to the child in ways that required assistance for the child to operate the toy. A train track was placed in front of the child with the experimenter holding the train in full view but out of reach and a garage with doors was presented with the keys that opened the doors out of reach. In addition, two jars holding windup toys were placed on the table with the tops screwed on so tightly that the child could not remove them without help. In order to elicit the initiation of joint attention, windup toys were placed in front of the child as in the original version of the ESCS. In addition, a mechanical seal that made noises was surreptiously activated on the floor and a remote-control light placed behind the experimenter was turned on. Response to joint attention was measured in terms of the child's reactions to the experimenter's pointing, as in the earlier assessment, as well as in response to the experimenter's gaze. The administration of the scales was videotaped and the child's nonverbal responses were coded in the same way as had been done earlier. We did not attempt to elicit or code the initiation or response to social interaction but limited the coding to the frequency of initiation of joint attention and requesting and responses to bids for joint attention, coded as percentage scores. According to interclass correlations, reliability on 18 cases was good, $rs$ (16) = .93, .90, and .88 for initiates joint attention, responds to bids for joint attention, and initiates behavior regulation respectively.

The scale was administered to 122 children at follow-up, 36 children with autism, 61 children with Down syndrome, and 25 children with developmental delays. The language ages of the three groups were equivalent, $p > .12$. The results of the group comparisons were similar to the results when the children were younger; there were significant group differences in the frequency of initiating joint attention and behavior regulation and in the percentage of responding to bids for joint attention, $F(2, 119) = 6.72$, $p < .002$, $F(2, 119) = 4.99$, $p < .01$, and $F(2, 119) = 3.46$, $p < .04$, respectively.

According to the Newman-Keuls tests, the children with autism initiated joint attention and behavior regulation less than the children in the other two groups; autism group less than Down syndrome group, $ps < .01$ and $< .03$, respectively; autism group less than developmentally delayed group, $ps$ $< .02$ and .02, respectively. The children with autism also responded to bids for joint attention less than the developmentally delayed group, $p < .02$, but did not differ from the children with Down syndrome. Therefore, at follow-up, the children with autism were somewhat more deficient in behavior regulation and somewhat less deficient in the capacity to respond to bids for joint attention than at intake.

In terms of individual continuity, the extent to which the children with autism and the children with developmental delays initiated joint attention was significantly correlated across the two time points, $r(27) = .47$, $p < .01$, and $r(20) = .45$, $p < .04$, with initial mental age and language age covaried. This was not true for their frequency of initiating behavior regulation or responding to joint attention nor was it true for any of the nonverbal communication skills for the children with Down syndrome. Thus, the group differences in nonverbal communication remained stable over time but individual continuity was manifested only by the autistic and developmentally delayed children in terms of the extent to which they initiated joint attention.

### Continuity and Change in Language Abilities Over Time

Another question addressed was about group change in language abilities over time. At follow-up, children who were able to show basal level scores on the vocabulary test of the Stanford-Binet were administered the Childhood Evaluation of Language Fundamentals-Revised (CELF-R; Semel, Wiig, & Secord, 1987). Children who were unable to reach basal levels on this instrument were administered the Reynell Scales and the preschool version of the Childhood Evaluation of Language Fundamentals (Wiig, Secord, & Semel, 1992). Because more children were tested with the Reynell Scales than any other measure, these scales were included in analyses if they had been administered.

Only 25 children (14 with autism, 3 with Down syndrome, and 8 with developmental delays) were administered the CELF-R, whereas 100 children were administered the Reynell Scales. Both measures furnish age-equivalent scores. For the three participants who were older than the standardization sample, these were calculated using the oldest age given, 17 years. Both measures separate the assessment of receptive and expressive language abilities. Since these are given as age scores in the Reynell, the Standardized Assessment Scores on the CELF, which have a mean of 100 and a standard deviation of 15, were multiplied by the child's age to give estimates of receptive and expressive language ages that could be used in analyses along with the Reynell receptive and expressive language ages.

In order to determine the extent of gain in language skills and to compare this gain across groups, a 3 (Group) × 2 (Time of testing) ANOVA was conducted. There was a significant Group × Time interaction, $F(2, 130) = 3.25, p < .04$. The three groups of children did not differ in language skills at initial testing but did differ at follow-up, $F(2, 212) = 9.40, p < .001$. The children with developmental delays had higher language skills at follow-up than the other two groups, who did not differ from each other (see Table 10).

In terms of change over time, all the groups showed increases in mean language ages although very much less than would be expected for typically developing children. At follow-up, some 8–9 years after intake, the mean gain in language age was 28 months for the children with autism, 23 months for the children with Down syndrome, and 36 months for the children with developmental delays. Furthermore, a comparison of the gain in language

TABLE 10

LANGUAGE AGES IN YEARS AND MONTHS AT INTAKE AND FOLLOW-UP

| | | Autistic Group $n = 41$ | Down Syndrome Group $n = 61$ | Developmental Delay Group $n = 31$ |
|---|---|---|---|---|
| Initial Language Ages | Mean | 1–6 | 1–7 | 2–0 |
| | SD | .74 | .53 | .92 |
| Follow-Up Language Age | Mean | 3–10 | 3–6 | 5–0* |
| | SD | 2.69 | 1.43 | 2.15 |

*Significantly different from the other two groups, which do not differ from each other, $p < .05$.

skills across time showed that the amount of gain made by the developmentally delayed children was higher than for the other two groups.

The differential between expressive and receptive languages was insignificant for the children with autism at both time points. Receptive language was significantly higher than expressive language for the developmentally delayed children at intake, $t(48) = 2.42$, $p < .02$, but not at follow-up. At intake, the difference was 1.55 months; mean receptive language age was 20.67 months ($SD = 7.30$) and mean expressive language age was 19.12 months ($SD = 6.76$). The receptive language scores of the children with Down syndrome were higher than their expressive language scores at both ages, $t(92) = 3.46$, $p < .001$ at intake and $t(58) = 2.68$, $p < .01$, at follow-up. At neither age was the difference very large. At intake, the difference was 1.75 months; mean receptive language age was 18.95 months ($SD = 7.27$) and mean expressive language age was 17.20 months ($SD = 5.28$). At follow-up, the difference was still only 4.2 months for the children with Down syndrome; mean receptive language age was 44.32 months ($SD = 17.3$) while mean expressive language age was 40.17 months ($SD = 19.7$). Thus, the productive language of the children with Down syndrome was less advanced than their receptive language but both receptive and expressive language skills were delayed.

Correlations between initial and follow-up language ages were calculated for the three groups of children. As would be expected, early language age predicted later language age. The correlations (with initial chronological age covaried) are $r(39) = .56$, $r(59) = .49$, and $r(29) = .71$ for the children with autism, Down syndrome, and developmental delay respectively. In contrast to the developmentally delayed group who evidenced equal stability in receptive and expressive language, the stability of receptive language was somewhat higher than for expressive language for the autistic group, $r = .61$ versus .51.

For the children with Down syndrome, the predictions were even more different for receptive and expressive language. The correlation between early and later receptive language ages was $r(57) = .54$ in contrast to $r(57) = .23$ for early and later expressive language. Thus, early expressive language skills did not predict later expressive language skills for the children with Down syndrome. This may have been because the expressive language skills assessed at intake were largely prelinguistic. Evidence to support this hypothesis is that receptive language age at intake predicted expressive language age at follow-up in the Down syndrome sample, $r(57) = .58$, $p < .0001$.

Lord and Schopler (1989a) have examined the continuity of language skills in children with autism by defining the criterion for the beginning of language understanding as a receptive language age of 23 months. Using the same criterion as Lord and Schopler (1989a), 9 of 41 children with autism demonstrated some understanding of language at recruitment and follow-up, 23 children did not understand language at recruitment but did so at follow-up, and 9 children never demonstrated understanding of verbal labels. Replicating the findings of Lord and Schopler (1989a), the intelligence level of the children with autism who gained an understanding of language did not differ initially from the intelligence level of the children who never came to understand language (although both groups were less intelligent initially than the children who started the study with an understanding of language). The results were similar for the two studies despite the fact that the earlier study used a nonverbal measure of intelligence whereas the current study used a general measure of intelligence. Thus, early assessments of intelligence do not seem to be predictive of later language skills in children with autism whose receptive language abilities are less than 23 months.

*Predictions of Language Gains From Nonverbal Communication Skills*

Just as early communicative and play skills are expected to be associated with language abilities in children, so it is reasonable to think that these abilities might underlie the child's capacities to expand on their language learning after the period of language acquisition. In order to examine the contribution of nonverbal communication and play skills to language gains, the correlations of nonverbal communication behaviors and follow-up language scores with initial chronological and language ages partialled out of the correlations were computed. There was a nearly significant association between response to joint attention and language gain for the children with autism, $r (33) = .33, p < .053$. For the children with autism, rate of responding to bids for joint attention predicted gain in expressive language age, $r(33) = .46, p < .01$, and not gain in receptive language age. Frequency of requesting was predictive of language gains (both in receptive and expressive language skills) for the children with developmental delays, $rs(25) = .60$ and $.58, p < .002$. For the children with Down syndrome, gains in expressive language skills were predicted by social interaction behaviors. Children who initiated social interactions somewhat more, $r(49) = .27, p < .06$, and responded to social interactions less, $r(49) = -.32, p < .02$, made bigger long-term gains in expressive language abilities.

*Prediction of Language Gains From Representational Play Skills*

Play skills did not predict long-term gains when overall language abilities were assessed. However, the number of different functional acts predicted gains in expressive language age for the children with autism. Children who engaged in more functional play initially improved more in expressive language skills than children whose functional play was more

47

impoverished initially, $r(37) = .33$, $p < .04$. Improvement in receptive language skills was not predicted by earlier play skills. Functional play may have been more predictive than symbolic play because of the broader range of functional play acts or because the very high concurrent association between early symbolic play and language scores limited the contribution of early symbolic play when early language scores were entered into the partial correlation as a covariate. Although representational play behaviors predicted short-term gain in language skills for the developmentally delayed children, this was not true for long-term gain in language skills.

As the number of different functional play acts and the percentage of responses to bids for joint attention were correlated for the autistic sample, two hierarchical regressions were calculated with expressive language age at follow-up as the dependent variable and expressive language age at intake entered first into the regression. If response to joint attention was entered first, then the number of different functional play acts did not enter into the regression and the amount of the variance accounted for was 38%. If the number of different functional play acts was entered first, then response to joint attention also entered and the amount of variance in expressive language gain accounted for was 43%. Thus, both variables predict independently the gain in expressive language made by children with autism although nonverbal communication skills contribute more to this prediction.

*Predictions of the Change in Mental Retardation for the Children With Autism*

As described in Chapter II, one of the most striking findings in this study is that a considerable number of children with autism who test as mentally retarded made significant enough gains in intelligence to be considered high-functioning at the time of the follow-up. As shown in Table 3, 11 children showed this pattern of change so that 14 of the 43 children who were tested could be considered high-functioning at follow-up. A very important question from the point of view of potential interventions is what accounts for this change in level of intelligence. In order to answer this question, the nonverbal communication and play scores of the children who scored below 70 IQ initially and remained below at follow-up were compared with the nonverbal communication and play skills of those children who scored below 70 initially and rose above 70 at follow-up. The results showed that the children who moved out of the mentally retarded group responded more to bids for joint attention, $F(1,32) = 5.39$, $p < .03$, requested objects or assistance with objects more, $F(1,32) = 4.77$, $p < .04$, and demonstrated different functional play acts more, $F(1,37) = 4.43$, $p < .04$, than the children who remained in the mentally retarded group.

One possible interpretation of this result is that children who were more intelligent initially were more likely to make this change, because nonverbal communication scores were correlated with intelligence at intake. In order to determine whether this was so, chronological age and intelligence were compared for the children who stopped being mentally retarded and those who remained mentally retarded. There was no significant difference in chronological age in the two groups but there was in intelligence. Covarying initial intelligence, however, only altered the findings for representational play. The children who remained retarded differed from those who became high-functioning in terms of their initial frequency of requesting behaviors and ability to follow pointing behaviors.

## DISCUSSION

This examination of the aggregated data confirms some of our previous findings and disconfirms others. The results confirm that young children with autism suffer from a deficit in joint attention that is unique to children with autism. Children with other developmental disorders look to other people to share their experiences and follow the gaze of others as much as normal children. Only autistic children fail to attend jointly, show objects to others, point to objects and people, and track the pointing and eye gaze of others. Moreover, the deficit is specific in that the children with autism are not different in all forms of social communication. Whereas they request objects less than some of the other children, the differential in requesting behaviors is much smaller than in joint attention. In structured situations like this one, they initiate and respond to social bids as much as the other groups.

Children with autism also demonstrate limitations in their symbolic play although the group differences are smaller than we have previously reported with smaller samples. The reasons for these differences in findings may be threefold. First, the limitations in the functional play skills of children with autism are most apparent in unstructured settings. The observations used here are of the children's play when they are seated opposite an experimenter who confines the children's movements, keeps the children engaged with the toys, and tries to optimize the children's play behaviors. The play of autistic children appear most dysfunctional when they are free to wander around with little adult supervision. The diminution in group differences as a function of structure supports the notion that children with autism are able to play functionally and symbolically in a more mature fashion than they often demonstrate.

Second, differences in play are minimized when children with autism and control groups are matched closely on language skills, rather than general developmental skills. Whereas matching on language age is appropriate from the point of view of experimental design, a defining criterion for autism is serious language delay. Other developmentally disabled children do not usually have such impoverished language skills. Therefore, group matching on language abilities distorts the situation from a clinical viewpoint. The absence or paucity of play is very useful in the clinical differentiation of autism from other developmental disorders.

The third reason why the play difference may be smaller than previously reported is that the developmentally delayed group is separated from the Down syndrome group. In all our previous work on autism, the control group consisted of equal numbers of developmentally delayed and Down syndrome children. It is clear from the current analysis that the children with Down syndrome have superior play abilities. Therefore, the inclusion of these children in the control group may have magnified the limitations in play skills of the children with autism.

Children with Down syndrome obviously have no problems with symbolic play and they do not even appear to suffer from a unique deficit in nonverbal communication. Whereas they request objects and assistance less than normal children, as we have previously reported, this is true for all the developmentally disordered groups and, therefore, is not unique to Down syndrome. In general, the children with Down syndrome seem to communicate nonverbally rather well and their play skills are remarkable. The observation that the children with Down syndrome engage in more functional and symbolic play than normal children of equal mental and language age suggests that their representational awareness is superior to what is reflected in the assessments of their language abilities.

The major area of deficit for the children with Down syndrome is in language skills. Their expressive language scores are significantly worse than their receptive language scores both early and later in childhood, and their early expressive language ability has no bearing on their later expressive language skills. Congruent with these results are the findings that children with Down syndrome show more lexical understanding than is true for normal children in the same language stage (Mervis, 1988). Nonverbal communication and play behaviors are associated with concurrent early language skills (although not as strongly as seen with the other developmentally disabled groups) and nonverbal communication behaviors are predictive of later gains in language.

One of the new findings from this reexamination of the data is that the nonverbal communication and play behaviors that are concurrently associated with language skills are similar for all the groups investigated. The major correlates are joint attention and representational play. In previous reports, we identified an association between requesting behaviors and language skills for the children with Down syndrome, an association that is maintained with this larger data set. This association, however, is smaller in magnitude than the correlations between language and joint attention behaviors and the frequency of requesting is not predictive of language skills over time in the Down syndrome group.

The failure of children with Down syndrome to develop their language abilities does not seem to stem to a very great extent from deficits in nonverbal communication and symbolic understanding. Whereas these abilities are correlated with language skills, the associations are somewhat weaker than those in the autistic and developmentally delayed samples.

Many other researchers have found that children and adults with Down syndrome have very limited syntactic development, lagging behind what would be expected in terms of their mental age (Fowler, Gelman, & Gleitman, 1994; Miller, 1988). Limitations in productive language overshadow deficits in other forms of language. At the same time, language seems to develop in the same way in children with Down syndrome as in typically developing children, albeit at a slower rate. Delays in the initiation and stability of canonical babbling in the 1st year of life may point to motor difficulties, as well as cognitive limitations, that underlie this expressive language disorder (Lynch et al., 1995). On the other hand, the delay in canonical babbling is not the rule among infants with Down syndrome in contrast to the later pronounced delays in expressive language. As one research group has noted (Fowler et al., 1994), the dilemma is twofold: why children with Down syndrome learn over 12 years what infants acquire in 30 months and why most of them fail to acquire the complex syntax that their mental abilities would suggest that they could master.

The one area in which all the developmentally disabled children differ from the normal children is in the frequency with which they attempt to regulate the behavior of others to obtain a toy or assistance with a toy. This could mean that mentally retarded children do not understand how to use other people to obtain what they want as well as normal children. Most studies that have compared the understanding of means-ends relationships, however, do not report differences between mentally retarded and normal children when the groups are matched on mental age (Weisz & Zigler, 1979). Therefore, this lack of understanding would have to apply only to the instrumental use of other people.

Another interpretation is that mentally retarded children are less interested in object manipulation and mastery and, therefore, less motivated to use other people to obtain objects or assistance with objects. This interpretation suggests that a cause as well as a consequence of being less successful with objects and tasks is that one is less interested in mastering them. In a number of studies, children with Down syndrome were less engaged with mastery tasks than control children (Berry, Gunn, & Andrews, 1984; Brooks-Gunn & Lewis, 1982; Krakow & Kopp, 1983; Landry & Chapieski, 1990; Ruskin, Kasari, et al., 1994; Ruskin, Mundy, et al., 1994) but this was not true in all studies (MacTurk, Vietze, McCarthy, McQuiston, & Yarrow, 1985). In our own research, children with Down syndrome were less engaged with mastery tasks and showed less pleasure in achieving their goals than typically developing children. Neither the degree of persistent goal directed behavior with toys nor pleasure in achieving goals, however, was associated with the frequency of requesting behaviors. For this reason, the deficit in requesting does not seem to index a deficiency in mastery motivation.

An important set of questions about children with Down syndrome is whether they show more interest in interacting with other people than other children of their mental abilities and whether this interest in social participation is at the expense of their task mastery. Several studies have shown that children with Down syndrome look more at the faces of their social partners and less at toys (Brooks-Gunn & Lewis, 1982; Kasari, Freeman, Mundy, & Sigman, 1995; Kasari, Mundy, Yirmiya, & Sigman, 1990; Landry & Chapieski, 1990). These very protracted periods of attention to the face of another person may be in the service of trying to understand the other person as the children with Down syndrome who are most attentive to the adult's face are frequently the less cognitively competent children (Kasari et al., 1990, 1995).

In a study in which social participation was alternated with toy presentation, children with Down syndrome looked more to the experimenter but not to the toy than typically developing children (Ruskin, Mundy, et al., 1994). They also spent more time singing a song with the experimenter, smiled more during the singing, and rejected the toys more than the typically developing children. As a group, then, the children with Down syndrome were more engaged with the experimenter and less with the toys than the typically developing children. On an individual level, however, social participation did not replace task engagement. Children with Down syndrome who participated more in the social game and demonstrated more pleasure while doing so also were more engaged in goal directed activity with the toys and showed more pleasure in this activity. Moreover, both social participation and task engagement characterized the more cognitively and linguistically competent children with Down syndrome. Thus, the social enthusiasm of the children with Down syndrome is not expressed at the cost of their task mastery and seems advantageous for their cognitive and linguistic development.

The results show that nonverbal communication and play skills are concurrently linked to language skills. Limitations in comparing and interpreting correlational data need to be discussed. The extent to which behaviors are correlated in any sample depends on a variety of factors, including the range of the behaviors shown by any sample and the size of the sample. It may be more difficult to identify associations in samples where a behavior is at basal or ceiling levels, although the significant correlations between the joint attention behaviors and language scores (which are both low in the autistic sample) show that it is not impossible.

There is a second source of difficulty in interpreting predictions to language abilities in this study. Because outcome language abilities are a function of intake language abilities, the latter have to be controlled statistically in determining whether nonverbal communication and play skills predict gains in language. The associations between intake nonverbal communication and play skills with language scores, however, are not equivalent for all of the nonverbal communication, play, and language skills so that statistical covariation operates differently across different skills. For example, there is a higher correlation at intake between the symbolic play measure and language skills than is true for the functional play measure and language skills for the children with autism. Whereas the simple correlations between intake functional and symbolic play with long-term follow-up language scores are equivalent, only the association between functional play and language scores is significant once intake language age is covaried. This is probably due to the fact that more of the variance in early language scores is explained by early symbolic play so that covariation of early language scores leaves less shared variance to be explained by later symbolic play than is true for functional play. The same explanation also may pertain to the differential prediction of expressive and receptive language skills by early joint attention and functional play skills in the autistic sample.

The results of this longitudinal study depend on correlational analyses to uncover paths of development. Correlational studies can never furnish information about causality so that experimental studies are needed to determine whether changes in nonverbal communication and play skills lead to improved language acquisition. The enhancement of nonverbal communication and play skills in children with autism through intervention programs might have not only short-term consequences for their language acquisition but might even affect their later developmental course. We will return to this theme in Chapter VI of this monograph, in which we discuss the predictors of peer interactions skills in the developmentally disabled children followed into the mid-school years.

# IV. SOCIAL AND EMOTIONAL RESPONSIVENESS

Social and emotional responsiveness are critical components of social competence. Individuals who do not understand the reactions of others are unable to form satisfying relationships. In addition, some individuals are able to understand others but do not respond appropriately and this, too, interferes with their social lives.

The evidence that children with autism do not engage in joint attention led us to investigate the extent to which the children reacted to the emotional displays of others. Our original reason for doing this was that it seemed possible that children with autism would show more joint attention in emotionally charged situations where the stimulus was stronger. Thus, the children with autism might look at others less when exploring toys simply because it did not occur to them to do so but they might be more attentive to others in situations where the others were showing strong emotions.

A series of studies conducted to address this question has shown that the attention of children with autism to other people is not normalized when the person with whom the child is interacting shows strong emotions. In the first of these studies, the behaviors of young children with autism to the familiar caregiver or the experimenter pretending to feel pain, pleasure, discomfort, or fear were observed (Sigman et al., 1992). There were no group differences in affects expressed in that few of the children showed much emotion. The children with autism, however, looked much less at the person showing pain, spent much more time playing with a toy that the experimenter had been using, and appeared far less interested and concerned than children with mental retardation and normal controls. This was true whether the person showing pain was the caregiver or the experimenter. Thus, the hypothesis that an intense display of affect might normalize the attention of the children with autism was not supported. Moreover, the results raised the question whether the affect of others was responsible for suppressing the attention of children with autism, a view held by those who see autism as involving an aversion for interpersonal contact.

In order to test this hypothesis, a separate study of a new sample of young children with autism and a mentally retarded control group was conducted (Corona, Dissanayake, Arbelle, Wellington, & Sigman, 1998). In this study, the children were exposed to an experimenter who pretended to hurt her knee in both of two testing sessions. In one session, the experimenter showed strong distress whereas in the other session the experimenter showed neutral affect. The results showed that young children in both groups looked more and were rated as more interested and concerned about the experimenter when she showed strong distress than when she showed neutral affect. The children with autism attended less than the mentally retarded children to the person showing both distress and neutral affect. Thus, autistic children seem to attend less to people regardless of their emotional displays and the affect of others is not responsible for this lesser interest.

In both of these studies, the reactions of children with autism were contrasted with the responses of a heterogeneous control group including both children with Down syndrome and children with other developmental delays. Given the popular view and our own evidence that children with Down syndrome are very engaged in social interactions (Ruskin, Kasari, et al., 1994), the difference in social attention between the children with autism and the control group of mentally retarded children might be due to the high social attentiveness of the children with Down syndrome rather than the low social attentiveness of the autistic children. The availability of the larger data set enabled us to reexamine these findings, separating the data for the Down syndrome and developmentally delayed groups. In this way, it could be determined whether the group differences were due to the high social attentiveness of children with Down syndrome or the low social attentiveness of children with autism.

## EMOTIONAL RESPONSIVENESS AT INITIAL ASSESSMENT

The reactions of the children to the experimenter's distress was observed when the two of them were seated at a small table. The experimenter, while playing with a wooden pounding toy and small hammer, pretended to hurt her finger by hitting it with the hammer. She then displayed vocal and facial expression of distress. Following 10 seconds of neutral affect, the experimenter reassured the child by showing that her finger did not hurt anymore.

The experimenter and the child were videotaped during this procedure and both individual's behaviors were coded from the videotape. Continuous coding was conducted of the child's attention to the experimenter's face and the child's engagement with the toy. Distress episodes varied in duration across the sample so the behavioral data were transformed into percentage scores. In addition, the child's interest and concern for the experimenter was measured using a 6-point empathy rating scale: (1) shows no interest, (2) shows a hint of interest, (3) shows some apparent interest but no clear concern, (4) shows one sign of concern, (5) shows more than one sign of concern, and (6) shows intense affective involvement and/or comforting behavior. Reliability as reported in Sigman et al. (1992) was $\kappa$ = .86 for attention counted in half seconds, $\kappa$ = .95 for toy play, and $\kappa$ = .76 for the rating scale. An independent observer rated the intensity of the experimenter's demonstrations of affect and there were no group differences.

### Group Differences in Response to the Experimenter's Distress

In order to determine if there were group differences in emotional reactions, the percentage of time that the child attended to the experimenter's face and played with the toy as well as the interest/concern rating were compared across groups. A preliminary analysis indicated that the four groups who were administered the response to distress measures did not differ in language age, $p$ > .20. As there was a significant group effect on the MANOVA calculated on the three measures combined, Wilk's $\lambda$ = .52, $F(9, 355.4)$ = 12.08, $p$ < .0001, separate ANOVAs were calculated for each measure. The results confirmed the previous findings that children with autism were less responsive to the distress of others. There were group differences in looking at the experimenter, $F(3, 147)$ = 23.86, $p$ < .00001, and playing with the toy, $F(3, 150)$ = 17.63, $p$ < .00001. Post hoc analyses demonstrated that these differences were attributable to the behavior of the children with autism. They looked far less at the experimenter's face than the other children, $M$ = 24% versus $M$ = 64%, 60%, and 69%; autistic group less than all other groups, $p$ < .0001, according to the Newman-Keuls test. They also played far more with the toy, $M$ = 73% versus $M$ = 17%, 22%, and 21%, autistic group greater than all other groups, $p$ < .0001, according to the Newman-Keuls tests. In addition, the groups differed on the empathy ratings, $F(3, 145)$ = 7.98, $p$ < .0001. Surprisingly, both the children with autism and the children with Down syndrome had lower empathy ratings than the developmentally delayed and normal children, $M$ = 2.89 for the autistic children, $M$ = 3.15 for the Down syndrome group, $M$ = 4.80 for the developmentally delayed group, and $M$ = 4.04 for the normal group (autistic group less than developmentally delayed group, $p$ < .0002, autistic group less than normal group, $p$ < .02, Down syndrome group less than developmentally delayed group, $p$ < .0004, Down syndrome group less than normal group, $p$ < .03, according to the Newman-Keuls test).

The findings for the children with autism confirmed our previous results in that the children with autism were much less responsive than the other groups. Moreover, this group difference was clearly not attributable to the children with Down syndrome who, unexpectedly, had lower empathy ratings than the children in the developmental delayed and normal groups and equivalent ratings to the children in the autistic group. Thus, the group differences previously reported were clearly due to the low social attentiveness of the children with autism and not due to the behaviors of the children with Down syndrome.

## SOCIAL AND EMOTIONAL RESPONSIVENESS AT FOLLOW-UP

The investigation of emotional and social responsiveness was an important goal of the follow-up study. One aim was to determine whether children with autism continued to be less responsive to the affects of others as they matured. As mentioned previously, children with autism change with development and often seem to become more socially interested as they grow older, although this has not been studied systematically. The follow-up study was designed to examine the reactions of this older group of autistic, Down syndrome, and developmentally delayed children to others' distress and anger as well as to social situations in which prosocial behaviors were elicited. The display of anger was used as a stimulus to determine the generality of the older children's reactions to different affects. The prosocial situations were added to the protocol to broaden the range of behaviors examined in this study to include those appropriate for social situations which occur frequently in everyday life. Our hypothesis was that, in contrast to the other two groups, children with autism would show less attention to the distress and anger of others as well as less helping and sharing behavior in a social situation that elicited these behaviors.

It was more difficult to formulate hypotheses about the behavior of children with Down syndrome. As mentioned above, high degrees of social attention and concern have been noted in children with Down syndrome so it seemed likely that they would continue to be at least as responsive and helpful (and possibly more so) than the children with developmental delays. The only evidence to the contrary was our somewhat idiosyncratic observation that the children were rated as less interested and concerned at the distress of others than was true for the developmentally delayed children.

An additional purpose of this follow-up was to determine whether the children with Down syndrome and developmental delays showed stability in response to others' distress as we have previously reported for this sample of children with autism (Dissanayake, Sigman, & Kasari, 1996). Preliminary coding of the follow-up data from only the autistic sample was carried out to determine whether there was long-term stability in the reactions to others' distress in children with autism. (It should be mentioned that these are the only data published at this time from the follow-up study.) Using a similar coding system with the autistic sample to the one described before, total duration of looking to the experimenter and empathy scores during the experimenter distress procedure predicted empathy scores in the follow-up distress procedure. This association remained significant even when intake mental age was covaried. Thus, the autistic children who were more emotionally responsive at age 3–5 years also were more responsive later. The coding of the data from the autistic sample was carried out before the data collection from the other groups was completed so the groups were not compared nor was stability in the other groups examined. For this reason, the extent of stability in emotional responsiveness among the children with Down syndrome and developmental delays has not been assessed so that we do not know if response to distress is stable in these groups as well.

A final goal of the follow-up was to investigate social understanding in the children with autism, Down syndrome, and developmental delays. Unfortunately, only about one third of the sample had sufficient language skills to comprehend and respond to the measures of social understanding. For this reason, the sample sizes are small so that these data are not included in this monograph.

## Group Differences in Social Responsiveness

### Prosocial Behaviors

Cooperative and helping behaviors were measured by providing the child with opportunities to assist the experimenter during a social interaction in which juice, cookies, and candy were served. The experimenter entered the room with a tray full of refreshments and approached the child, who was seated at a small table that was almost completely covered with other objects. The experimenter waited for the child to remove some objects spontaneously from the table so that the experimenter could place the tray on the table. A second opportunity for helping behavior was provided when the experimenter spilled some juice while pouring and waited for the child to assist in cleaning it up. In both these situations, the experimenter prompted the child to provide help if the child did not offer assistance spontaneously. In each situation, helping behavior was coded from the videotape with a 4-point scale ranging from (1) no help even after both hinting and asking to (4) unsolicited helping behaviors. Interrater reliability was good, $\kappa s = .82$ and $.91$, for the rating scale in the two situations.

To tap the child's tendency to share with others, two procedures were used. In one, the experimenter waited to see if the child would spontaneously offer the experimenter any cookies or juice before prompting, "Gee, I sure am hungry" and then finally, "May I have some?" In the second procedure, an experimenter entered the room with some photos of animals that he or she exclaimed over and then handed to the child to look at. The first experimenter demonstrated interest in looking at the photos by craning her neck in the direction of the photos. The experimenter waited to see if the child would show the experimenter the photos before suggesting that they do so. Sharing behaviors were rated with scales like the one described for helping behaviors. Interrater reliabilities were good, $\kappa$s = .79 and .85. The ratings were combined across situations to make one rating of sharing behaviors.

This measure was administered to the 43 autistic participants, 63 of the 66 participants with Down syndrome, and 30 of the 33 participants with developmental delays who were seen for testing in the follow-up sample. The procedure could not be administered to six participants who were tested in institutions or at home and some parts of the procedures were not administered to the initial participants. The data from the four most advanced children with developmental delays were excluded from analyses in order to equate the groups on language age, $p > .14$.

Ratings of cooperative behavior with the tray, helping to clean up the spill, and sharing behaviors were compared across groups in a MANOVA that was significant according to Wilk's criterion, Wilk's $\lambda$ = .90, $F(6,242)$ = 2.11, $p < .05$. There were significant group differences both in the rating of cooperating, $F(2,125)$ = 6.05, $p < .003$, as well as in the rating of sharing, $F(2,129)$ = 5.45, $p < .005$, but no significant group difference in rating of helping to clean up after the spill. The children with autism displayed fewer of the prosocial behaviors than either of the other two subject groups; autistic group less than Down syndrome group, $p < .009$ for cooperating, $p < .01$ for sharing, autistic group less than developmentally delayed group, $p < .009$ for cooperating, $p < .01$ for sharing, according to the Newman-Keuls test (see Figure 8).

In summary, our hypothesis that the children with autism would show fewer prosocial behaviors than the children in the other groups was supported. Children with autism were less likely to help with the tray, offer food, or share photos than other developmentally disabled children. The Down syndrome children were just as helpful as the developmentally delayed children. Thus, the children with Down syndrome show at least equivalent prosocial skills as the children with developmental delays.

### Response to Distress

The children's response to the experimenter's distress was observed using a procedure modified from that used at intake. During the social

59

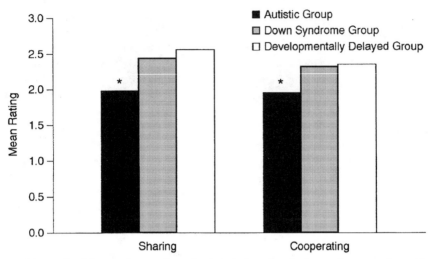

FIGURE 8.—Mean ratings and standard deviations for sharing and cooperating with the experimenter by children with autism, Down syndrome, and developmental delays. *Indicates that the children with autism shared and cooperated significantly less than the other groups.

interaction described above, the experimenter pretended to bump his or her knee on the table, exclaimed loudly, and feigned pain through facial expressions and body movements for 30 s. The experimenter then reassured the child that the knee felt better and showed neutral affect for 10 s. The child and experimenter were videotaped.

The total duration of the following child behaviors were coded: looks to the experimenter's face and orients away from the experimenter. These durations were converted to percentage scores to correct for any variability in the length of the procedure. The interrater reliability of these measures was good, $rs = .97$ and .99, respectively, using interclass correlations. In addition, the rating system used to measure interest and concern was changed from one 6-point rating system to two 3-point systems, one for interest and one for concern. This was done so that the child's level of interest could be judged separately from his or her level of concern. Reliability on the two rating systems was also good, $r = .80$ for interest and .93 for concern. Because of the changes in the coding system, the data from all participants were coded with this revised system and the preliminary coding of the behavior of the autistic children was replaced with the newly coded data.

To ensure that the experimenter's emotional displays were consistent for all three groups, the experimenter's performance was rated on its intensity and quality. Although analyses demonstrated no difference in the intensity of the affect displayed, there were group differences in the quality of the demonstration. Thus, data from all participants where the experimenter received a rating less than a 3 (the highest quality) were dropped from the analysis leaving 41 children with autism, 46 children with Down syndrome, and 21 children with developmental delays. For this group of participants there were no differences in language age, $p > .34$.

In order to determine whether the groups differed in their behavioral reactions to the distressed experimenter, separate ANOVAs were calculated for the two behavioral measures. There was a significant group difference only in the total duration that the child looked at the experimenter's face, $F(2, 103) = 15.59, p < .0001$. As was true when the children were younger, the children with autism looked to the experimenter's face for a smaller percentage of time than the other groups of children, $M = 21.6\%$ for the children with autism, $M = 42.6\%$ for the children with Down syndrome, and $M = 32.3\%$ for the children with developmental delays. The children with Down syndrome looked more and the children with autism looked less at the distressed experimenter than the other groups of children; autism group less than Down syndrome group, $p < .0001$, autism group less than developmentally delayed group, $p < .02$, developmentally delayed group less than Down syndrome group, $p < .02$. The groups did not differ in the proportion of time that they oriented away from the experimenter.

An ANOVA revealed that there were group differences in the global ratings of interest, $F(2,103) = 4.17, p < .02$, in that the children with Down syndrome were rated as more interested than the children with autism, $p < .05$ (see Figure 9). The Down syndrome children were clearly very interested in the experimenter's distress in that their rating was at the ceiling level.

There were also group differences in the global ratings of concern, $F(2,103) = 12.44, p < .0001$. A Newman-Keuls test showed that the children with autism were rated as less concerned than the other two groups; autism group less than Down syndrome group, $p < .0005$, autism group less than developmentally delayed group, $p < .0006$ (see Figure 9). It is important to note that, although the children with autism were less concerned, their level of interest was rated as no less than that of the children with developmental delays. Thus, the children with autism did seem engaged by the experimenter's demonstration of distress even though they looked less at the experimenter's face. They also gave no evidence of avoiding the distressed experimenter in that they did not orient away from him or her. In addition, the children with Down syndrome who had seemed less interested and concerned than the developmentally delayed children at the younger age were more interested and just as concerned at the older age.

UNIVERSITY OF HERTFORDSHIRE LRC

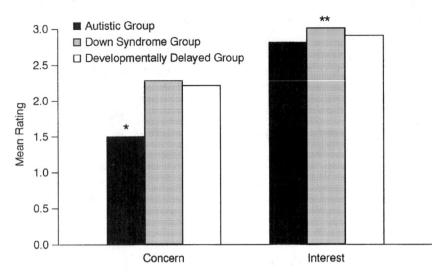

FIGURE 9.—Mean ratings and standard deviations for interest and concern shown toward an experimenter who pretended to have hurt herself and showed distress. *Indicates that the children with autism showed less concern than the children in the other groups. **Indicates that the children with Down syndrome showed more interest than the children with autism.

### Response to Anger

The children's reactions to an experimenter pretending to converse on the telephone were compared across groups. In one conversation, the experimenter pretended to be quite angry, whereas in the other she or he pretended to be more neutral in tone and expression. The order of the telephone conversations was counterbalanced across sessions. The loudness of the experimenter's voice was maintained at similar levels across both conversations. The child was videotaped during the conversations. The following behaviors were coded: looks to the experimenter and orients away from the experimenter. Interclass correlations for these measures were .91 and .90 respectively. In addition, the children's interest and concern were rated as described above.

Although there were no differences in the quality or intensity of the experimenter's performance for the phone call situations, data from all participants where the experimenter received a rating less than a 3 (the highest quality) were dropped from the analysis leaving 33 children with autism, 46 children with Down syndrome, and 20 children with developmental delays. For this group of participants there were no differences in language age, $p > .14$.

The angry situation used with the older children revealed somewhat unexpected results. The autistic children were the only group to differentiate between the two affects in terms of attention, orienting away, and ratings of interest. Thus, whereas there appeared to be a Conversation main effect in the overall 3 (Group) × 2 (Conversation) ANOVA, $F(1,96) = 6.52, p < .01$, only the autistic children looked longer at the experimenter when she pretended to be angry than when she was neutral, according to the simple main effects analysis, $F(1, 96) = 5.06, p < .03$. Moreover, there was a significant Group × Conversation interaction in the duration of orienting away from the experimenter, $F(2, 96) = 3.04, p < .05$. Autistic children oriented away more in the neutral than the angry condition, $F(1,96) = 5.19, p < .02$, but the children in the other two groups did not move away as a function of emotional tone of the conversation. The autistic children also oriented away more than the other children in the neutral conversation but not during the angry conversation. Finally, in the ratings of interest, the simple main effects analysis demonstrated that only the children with autism were significantly more interested in the angry experimenter than the neutral experimenter, $F(1, 96) = 8.90, p < .003$, although the differences were nearly significant for the other groups as well.

Thus, the anger of the experimenter seems to draw the attention and interest of the children with autism. At the same time, the attention of the autistic children was not normalized completely in that there was a significant group effect overall, $F(2, 96) = 8.02, p < .0006$. The children with autism looked at the adult pretending to talk on the telephone less during both conversations than the other children. Therefore, children with autism look less at all ages and in response to all kinds of emotional displays than other children of the same developmental level. The children with autism did not differ from the other children in either their interest or concern. All three groups showed far more concern when the experimenter was angry than when the experimenter was neutral in tone and facial expression, $F(1, 96) = 183.14, p < .00001$.

In summary, the older children with autism were less socially responsive to adults than other developmentally disabled children in that they were less cooperative and sharing. In addition, they continued to show less attention and orientation to the adult, whether the adult demonstrated distress, anger, or neutral affect. It is clear, however, that the autistic children can differentiate between emotions in that they looked more at an angry than a neutral adult and oriented away less from the angry than from the neutral adult. Moreover, the children with autism appeared as interested and concerned about the adult on the telephone as the other children although they were less concerned than the other children when the adult showed distress. There was no evidence that the children with autism avoid other people's affect. They simply seemed less drawn to attend to the faces of others, whether these others were showing strong affect or not.

The children with Down syndrome were very similar in their reactions to the developmentally delayed children. Although they were somewhat less empathic at an early age, this does not seem to remain true with development. Overall, they seemed neither more nor less responsive to the emotions and needs of others than other children with developmental disabilities.

## Associations Between Early and Later Social Responsiveness in Children With Down Syndrome

Given the lack of stability in the group differences in interest and concern in the Down syndrome group, a lack of individual continuity might also be expected. To address this issue, a Pearson product moment correlation was computed with mental age (MA) covaried between the duration of looking at the distressed experimenter at intake and at follow-up. Stability in empathy rating was not examined because the rating system was different at the two time periods. With the new coding system, duration of looking at the distressed experimenter was stable over time for the children with autism, $r(21) = .45$, $p < .03$, but not for the children with Down syndrome. There were only eight children with developmental delays seen at both time periods so stability in attention to the distressed experimenter was not examined in this group.

## DISCUSSION

In summary, the results show that children with autism are less attentive to the faces of others whatever the emotions of the other people. This was true whatever the age of the subject with autism. If the other person initiates social interaction as in the early social communication interaction discussed in Chapter III, the children with autism respond as much as other children. In situations where the initiation of attention is left up the children with autism, however, they are less attentive.

The deficit in attending to the faces of others appears to be a characteristic deficit in that it is unique to autism, universal in autism, and possibly specific to social stimuli. The deficit is unique to autism as children with Down syndrome and other developmental delays do not act similarly. The deficit seems to be universal in autism, being manifested by children and adolescents of all levels of ability and age. The extent to which the attentional deficit is general to all objects or specific to faces, however, is not clear. Young children with autism appear much less attentive to objects in totally unstructured play situations, although their attentiveness and interest increase when objects afford engaging interactions. Jigsaw puzzles are an example of the kind of objects with which autistic children can become totally engrossed. The specification of the deficit to social attention depends on equating the complexity and salience of social and nonsocial stimuli, a task that is very difficult to accomplish. Thus, the extent to which the deficit in attention is specific to people or more general is still unclear. Limitations in general attention regulation, however, characterize many childhood disorders so a deficit in attention is certainly not unique to autism.

One explanation for the lack of social attention of people with autism is the hypothesis that these individuals find social stimuli aversive and overarousing. There is no evidence from any of our studies to support this interpretation. At a young age, children with autism have been shown to look more at a person showing distress rather than neutral affect, and older children in this follow-up looked more and showed more interest in the angry experimenter than the neutral experimenter. The expression of affect drew their attention rather than repelling it. There is no evidence that the children with autism orient away from a distressed or angry experimenter; in fact, in the follow-up, the children oriented away from the neutral experimenter more than the angry experimenter.

The findings are in line with results from a study using heart rate change as a dependent measure (Corona et al., 1998). Heart rate of a mentally retarded, nonautistic control group decreased significantly compared to a baseline condition when the experimenter showed distress. Even when the experimenter pretended to have hurt her knee but did not show much affect, the decline in the heart rate of the mentally retarded in comparison to a baseline period was nearly significant. In contrast, the children with autism did not show a change in heart rate relative to the baseline condition in either condition. In other words, the autistic children did not orient to the social stimulus in the same way as the mentally retarded children. Perhaps even more important, the children with autism did not show an increase in heart rate that would be expected if the social stimuli were highly arousing and, therefore, aversive to them. Thus, the cardiac data support the behavioral findings that the children with autism react less to social signals but do not find them overarousing.

The responses of the Down syndrome sample parallel those of the developmentally delayed group. The finding of less empathy in the young children with Down syndrome in comparison to the developmentally delayed group needs to be replicated. Clearly, this same sample of children with Down syndrome is not less responsive in later life. The difference in the Down syndrome sample at the two age points may be due to the change in the rating scales used in this study or to an increase in social responsiveness within this group of children. The question as to whether children with Down syndrome are as skillful interpersonally as often believed will be addressed in the next two chapters on peer interactions.

# V. PEER INTERACTIONS IN SCHOOL

One goal of this monograph, discussed in Chapter I, is to examine several of the components of social competence in children with developmental disabilities. Two components of social competence—social communication and social responsiveness—have been discussed in previous chapters. A third component—the extent to which children engage in social interactions with peers—is the topic of the current chapter. Development of the capacity to initiate and maintain peer interactions is one of the most critical tasks of childhood. The acquisition of good peer interaction skills is fraught with difficulties for these developmentally disabled children.

## BACKGROUND

Evidence suggests that deficits in social participation exceed delays that would be expected based on a child's cognitive level, and that children with developmental disturbances are quite limited in their social interactions (Guralnick, 1986; Guralnick & Groom, 1985; Guralnick & Weinhouse, 1984; Strain, 1984). Guralnick and Groom (1985) demonstrated that the children with developmental disabilities in their sample spent the majority of time playing on their own, and less than 12% of the time engaged in social play; indeed only a small proportion of the children in their sample were responsible for half of these interactions. Observations of teachers, parents, and clinicians suggest that children with autism interact with peers even less than children with other developmental disabilities, although there has been little empirical documentation of these observations. Lord and Magill-Evans (1995) note that there has been little research on how children with autism interact with their peers in natural settings. One purpose of this study is to document whether these children are as uninvolved in social activities as is commonly believed.

*Peer Interactions of Children With Autism*

The peer interactions of the children with autism are likely to be so limited partly because of their lack of social capacities. Uta Frith (1989) in speaking of the "loneliness of the autistic child" notes that there is agreement over the social ineptness with which the individual with autism engages in two-way interactions. Individuals with autism had lower scores on the Vineland Adaptive Behavior Scale measure of interpersonal skills than either individuals with Down syndrome (Rodrigue, Morgan, & Geffken, 1991) or a developmentally delayed group matched on CA, gender, and IQ (Volkmar et al., 1987).

The knowledge that autistic children bring more limited interpersonal skills to peer interaction does not illuminate the behavioral deficits that children with autism show with peers. Children with autism may interact less with peers than other developmentally disabled children because they initiate interactions and respond to the invitations of others less frequently or because they are invited into play less by other children and have their initiations rebuffed more frequently. Thus, one possibility is that the children with autism may isolate themselves from others, whereas a second possibility is that the children with autism are interested in social interaction but are shunned by play partners. In addition, children with autism may maintain interactions for less time after a successful bid than is true for other children.

The deficits in dyadic interactions described in Chapters III and IV of this monograph suggests that autistic children are, at least partly, responsible for their own social isolation. The fact that they look so little at other people in one-to-one interactions must generalize to larger groups. For this reason, we would predict that children with autism would initiate interactions less than other developmentally disabled children, and there is evidence for this prediction. Hauck, Fein, Waterhouse, and Feinstein (1995) examined the quantity and nature of social initiations with peers and adults in children with autism. Children with autism initiated peer interactions much less frequently than language-matched children with developmental delays. In addition, the children with autism tended to greet or give information whereas the initiation bids of children with developmental delays were either to seek information or to enter into play. In line with this finding, Stone and Caro-Martinez (1990) showed that children with autism only communicated spontaneously about three to four times per hour during unstructured situations in school.

Children with autism also would be expected to respond less to others' invitations and maintain their own successful initiations for shorter periods given how difficult social interactions seem to be for them. On the other hand, the extent to which they suffer from involuntary isolation is less clear. One can imagine that other children might invite them into play less and reject their invitations more because of their previous experience of unsatis-fying interactions with the autistic children. There have been no investiga-tions of these patterns, however, so whether the other children are more tolerant than might be expected is not self-evident.

### Peer Interactions of Children With Down Syndrome

General impression as well as clinical description portrays children with Down syndrome as being particularly socially responsive but empirical re-search has yielded mixed findings regarding their level of sociability (Serafica, 1990). In our past research, children with Down syndrome have seemed particularly compelled by behavior of others, and indeed, by the human face in general. Our studies have revealed that children with Down syndrome spend significantly more time looking at an experimenter's face than toys (Kasari, Mundy, Yirmiya, & Sigman, 1990). During social referenc-ing situations, the children with Down syndrome fixated the face of a person modeling an emotion, rather than alternating attention between the actor and the eliciting object (Kasari, Freeman, Mundy, & Sigman, 1995). Children with Down syndrome also were more likely to participate in a social behavior (singing a song/doing hand motions with an experimenter), were more fo-cused in a social situation, and looked more frequently at the experimenter and less frequently away during social interaction than were typically devel-oping children (Ruskin, Kasari, et al., 1994). Given our findings of a deep in-terest in animated faces as well as the general impression of the friendliness of individuals with Down syndrome, we predicted that the children with Down syndrome would have a higher proportion of social interactions and would make and accept more social initiations than the group of children with developmental delays.

## CURRENT STUDY OF PEER INTERACTIONS

To determine whether there are group differences in peer interactions for the three groups of children, this study examined the level and quantity of peer interaction. Entry into social interaction was coded in terms of who initiated peer engagement (the subject or the peer), and in what light the ini-tiation was received (accepted or not accepted by partner) and whether in-teraction was maintained following an invitation. One aim of the current study was to document that autistic children are less involved in peer interac-tion than children with Down syndrome and children with developmental delays and that autistic children show more solitary and other nonsocial types of play than interactive play. A second aim was to compare the social interactions of the children with Down syndrome and the children with other developmental delays to determine whether children with Down syndrome are as or more involved in peer interactions than children of the same mental and language capacities but with different developmental disabilities. Because our hypotheses were less certain than those proposed in the earlier chapters of this monograph, a more conservative alpha level, $p <$ .01, was used in determining the significance of the results.

## Method

### Participants

The participants were 39 children with autism, 56 children with Down syndrome, and 29 children with other forms of developmental delay. As mentioned earlier, school data were not collected on the participants who lived outside of southern California. One of the local children with autism was not included in the study because his mother did not want him to be observed in school, and one of the local children with Down syndrome was not observed in school because she had no class or recess time that was suitable for our observation situations. In this second case, the teacher still completed a questionnaire about the child's popularity with their peer group.

As with the whole sample, the three subgroups differed on language age. When the four participants with the highest language ages in the group with developmental delays were excluded from the analyses, there were no longer any group differences in language age, $p > .10$. Thus, the analyses reported in the rest of the chapter do not include these four participants, reducing the sample size of the developmentally delayed group to 25 children.

The groups also differed in chronological age with the autistic children significantly older than the other two groups. Because of this, correlations between chronological age and each of the dependent variables were calculated. Chronological age was significantly correlated with three variables for the children with autism and with two variables for the children with Down syndrome. In these cases, the group comparisons were calculated with chronological age as a covariate. Chronological age was a significant covariate in one of the three analyses so that the results are reported with chronological age as a covariate only in that case.

### Procedures

During the initial laboratory visits, parents provided information regarding the name and location of the school as well as the name of the child's teacher. The teachers were then contacted by one of the researchers to schedule a school visit. Teachers were told that we did not want the child to know that he or she was being singled out for observation. Through the initial conversation with the teachers we determined the least structured time of day to observe social interaction, as well as a time in which we could observe the child in a more structured setting.

For the majority of the school visits, the child was observed on two separate days. Ten children with autism, five children with Down syndrome, and one child with developmental delay only received one school visit due to a very long commute or other scheduling problems. For these single visits, the researchers observed the child in an unstructured situation at two different times during the day, usually during morning and lunch or afternoon recess, and during two different types of classroom activities. Two of the children had more than two visits because of short recesses due to poor weather or special school events.

Each observation was scheduled to last for a minimum of 30 min. Observation times ranged from 31.75 min to 64.00 min, with a mean of 41.09 ($SD$ = 10.72) min. To account for the differences in observation times, all peer interaction data was transformed so that the frequency of a particular behavior was divided by the total amount of time that the child was observed. These proportions were used in the data analyses.

Each visit included an observation during a structured classroom activity and an unstructured recess time. The children were in a variety of different situations during the recess time. Thus, although we always tried to observe peer interaction in the least structured recess situation possible, some situations were inherently more structured than others. The children were observed during recess on the playground, free time in the classroom, lunch time, a physical education course, and other situations (e.g., one child had unstructured time in swimming pool with classmates).

Because the level of structure also varied across the different classrooms, experimenters rated the level of structure on the playground (or other unstructured time) and in the classroom (or other structured time) on a 5-point scale ranging from little organized structure to highly organized activities. Analyses of the global rating measure of structure revealed no overall group differences in the amount of structure in which the children were observed. Thus, the three diagnostic groups were observed during comparable situations.

## Peer Interaction Observation and Coding

### Level of Social Involvement

The measurement of peer interaction was based on the Peer Play Scale (Howes, 1980; Howes, 1987; Howes & Rodning, 1990). The behaviors that were coded to measure peer interaction levels are listed in Table 11. The level of peer interaction was coded continuously every 15 s. If more than one level was shown during a 15-s block, the highest level shown was recorded. Other interactive behaviors, such as initiations, responses, social activities, and vocalizations, were coded as they co-occurred in the 15-s blocks. In other words, these behaviors would be coded only once if they occured at all during the 15-s block. This means that the data for the behaviors represents the percentage of 15-s blocks in which the behavior was shown at least one time.

The methods for obtaining reliability on the peer interaction data will be discussed at length in a later section; only those behaviors that occurred frequently enough to be scored reliably are listed in Table 12. Some behaviors that could be observed reliably were so rare that they were dropped from analyses.

To reduce the number of variables in the study, the peer interaction level behaviors were combined. These combined variables represent four different levels of peer interaction: (1) nonsocial play (solitary, proximity, as well as onlooker near and far were combined to represent behaviors without a social component), (2) low level social play (parallel and aware play behaviors were combined as they contained an element of sociability without actual interaction), (3) high level social play (simple social play and organized games were combined into a total score of social behaviors), and (4) pretend play. Pretend play was so rare, however, that it was dropped from the analyses.

Smiling during high level social play suggests a particularly successful sort of social exchange. For this reason, a variable referred to as Social-

TABLE 11

DESCRIPTION OF LEVELS OF PEER INTERACTIONS

| 1. Solitary | The child plays alone, with no peers within 3 feet, and there is no mutual eye gaze with other children. |
|---|---|
| 2. Proximity | The child plays alone within 3-foot range of a peer. |
| 3. Onlooker/Near | The child has a one-way awareness of another child who is within a 3-foot range. |
| 4. Onlooker/Far | The child has a one-way awareness of a child who is farther away than 3 feet. |
| 5. Parallel | The child and a peer are engaged in a similar activity but there is no social behavior. |
| 6. Aware | The child and a peer are engaged in a similar activity and are mutually aware of each other during the activity. |
| 7. Simple Social | The child and a peer direct their social behavior, including offering objects, conversing, toy-taking, and other activities with a turn-taking structure. |
| 8. Games with Rules | The child participates in organized sports such as hopscotch or basketball. |

TABLE 12

INTERCLASS CORRELATIONS FOR PEER INTERACTION CODES

|  |  | Autistic | Down Syndrome | Developmentally Delayed | Total |
|---|---|---|---|---|---|
| Number |  | 10 | 10 | 8 | 28 |
| Percentage of Sample |  | 26% | 18% | 28% | 23% |
| Play Level | Nonsocial | 1.00 | .94 | 1.00 | .99 |
|  | Low Level | .99 | .98 | 1.00 | .99 |
|  | High Level | 1.00 | .97 | .96 | 1.00 |
|  | Social-Positive | 1.00 | .91 | .79 | .95 |
| Initiations | Child | .88 | .84 | .97 | .91 |
|  | Peer | 1.0 | .94 | .99 | .98 |
| Type of Entry | Accepted | .94 | .71 | .96 | .85 |
|  | Not accepted | .95 | .82 | .97 | .95 |
| Activity Type | Agonistic/physical | .35 | 1.00 | .99 | .91 |
|  | Respond/distress | .96 | No data | .98 | .97 |
|  | Respond/protest | .88 | 1.00 | .60 | .74 |
|  | Toy struggle | .91 | 1.00 | No data | .93 |
|  | Affection | 1.00 | 1.00 | .60 | .70 |
|  | Play organizer | 1.00 | No data | .00 | .99 |
|  | Rough and tumble | No data | No data | 1.00 | 1.00 |
| Vocalizations | Monologues | .99 | .86 | .79 | .95 |
|  | Conversations | 1.00 | .92 | .99 | .99 |
| Adult Roles | Initiate | .97 | .91 | .90 | .94 |
|  | Respond | .81 | .79 | .97 | .86 |
| Global | Structure (Kappas) | 1.00 | .70 | .82 | .85 |

Positive, comprised of high level social play that co-occurred with positive affect, was examined.

### Social Initiations

Getting started in social exchange is one of the most critical yet challenging aspects of peer interaction. Children have the daunting task of approaching another child (or group of children) and trying to organize a new activity or to integrate themselves into an ongoing activity. Otherwise, they need to be an appealing play partner so that others will invite them into play.

For these reasons, the coding of entry into play with another child was included as part of the observation. If the subject approached another child and tried to engage the peer in play, an initiation was coded for the subject ("subject-initiation"). If a peer approached the subject and tried to engage him or her in play then an initiation was coded for the peer ("peer-initiation").

### Response to Social Initiations

The subject- or peer-initiation was categorized in one of two ways: If the subject or the peer responded positively to the initiation and began to interact with the initiator, then the entry into play was coded as an "accept." If the subject or peer responded negatively to the interaction (the social bid was ignored or one of the children committed an agonistic act) then entry into play was coded as not accepted. For the most part, the type of play entry was coded in association with a subject- or peer-initiation, although not all play entries could be categorized in this way.

### Maintenance of Social Interactions

One question was whether a child could maintain an interaction once a social bid occurred. In addition to coding the proportion of subject-initiations and peer-initiations, it was necessary to examine the maintenance of interactions. Some children who rarely initiated social interactions played in isolation from the other children, whereas other infrequent initiators were involved with a single intense interaction throughout the play period. Some children initiated frequently but failed to maintain any interaction, whereas other children initiated frequently and kept up the social interaction for some amount of time. Thus, in order to differentiate between these patterns, we recorded the string of high level social behaviors that followed an initiation, and obtained a measure of average length of continuous high level social play following either subject-initiation or peer-initiation for each child.

### Social Activities

In addition to the level of social involvement, particular activities were observed and coded along with the levels of play. The observational categories for these social activities were based on measures used by Strain (1995). Although 22 behaviors were originally observed and recorded, many behaviors were so infrequent that it was impossible to establish reliability. Seven variables could be coded reliably for at least some of the subject groups: agonistic act, responds to agonistic act with distress, responds to agonistic act with protest, toy struggle, affection, organizes play, and rough and tumble play.

### Vocalizations

Talking to oneself is not likely to further an interaction with a peer whereas a conversation with another child is often a critical element of social exchange. The frequency with which a child carried on a monologue or participated in a conversation during the play time also was coded concurrently with the play behaviors.

### Interactions With Adults

In addition to interaction with peers, the frequency with which adults intervened or responded to a child's bid during recess was also noted. It was possible that some groups of children might be spending much of their playground time in interaction with adults rather than peers. Some groups of children may prefer to interact with adults rather than with peers. Children who are assisted frequently by adults, or who frequently initiate contact with adults, may have more difficulty in engaging in social relations with peers. Also, adults may initiate contact more with children who have disturbed social interaction abilities—either to try and integrate a child into an ongoing activity or to stop disruptive behaviors. In order to gain information about the role of adults on the playground, adult initiations and responses were coded separately.

### Reliability of Coding the Playground Interaction Variables

Training on the use of the peer interaction observation technique was carried out in three phases. In the first phase, the two researchers involved in data collection watched a tape provided by Carollee Howes to learn the Peer Play Scale. In the second phase, pilot studies were conducted in which the two researchers coded the behavior of children with autism, Down syndrome, and developmental delays who were not participants in this research. This coding continued until reliability was achieved. In the final phase, the two researchers collected reliability data on various children in the sample throughout the data collection period. Reliability was conducted on the three separate subject groups: There were 10 children in the autistic group (26% of the sample, $n = 39$), 10 children in the Down syndrome group (18% of the sample, $n = 56$) and 8 children in the developmentally delayed group (28% of the sample, $n = 29$). The reliability of the measures was quite good; the interclass correlations are presented in Table 12 for each of the groups as well as the three groups combined. All of the reliability figures are interclass correlations except for the ratings of structure, which are κs. For some of the individual activities, the frequencies for certain groups were too low to obtain reliability. In these cases, reliability figures for the whole group were generally high although these may have been inflated by the presence of zeroes. The data has been presented in the monograph as it seems important for both researchers and clinicians to be aware of the infrequency of these behaviors in the school setting.

*Teacher Rating of Peer Popularity*

In order to assess the teacher's view of how the child fit in with the social structure of the classroom, the teachers were asked to complete a peer popularity scale. Of the 124 students who participated in the school portion of the study, 95% had teachers who completed the peer popularity scale. The scale comprised 17 Likert-style ratings (Howes, 1987; Strain, 1984) that addressed the subject's popularity and ability to function among their peers. To account for the instances in which teachers skipped or missed a question, a mean rating was calculated across the 17 questions. The scale also contained two questions about the nature of the child's friendships (e.g., Does the subject have a best friend? and Does the subject have a group of friends?). Ninety percent of the teachers answered the questions about friends.

## GROUP DIFFERENCES IN PEER INTERACTIONS

*Level of Social Involvement*

The three diagnostic groups displayed different patterns in their peer interaction behaviors (see Table 13). A repeated measures ANOVA in which nonsocial play, low level play, and high level play were submitted as the dependent variables revealed a Group × Play Level interaction, $F(4,234) = 8.00$, $p < .0001$. Simple main effects analyses were conducted ($\alpha = .01$) and revealed that the children with autism displayed much more nonsocial play and less high level play than either the children with Down syndrome or the developmentally disabled groups. Within the group of children with autism, more nonsocial play was demonstrated than either low or high level play. Thus, play for the children with autism was characterized by nonsocial behavior. Our general impression was that many of the children with autism frequently spent the recess on the outskirts of the playground, either walking the perimeter of the school yard or remaining in one particular location by themselves for the entire recess. When left on their own (as children frequently are during recess) these children with autism frequently engaged in self-stimulating behaviors, such as watching their shadows, or shaking leaves, or using a toy in an inappropriate manner.

The children with developmental delays showed a contrasting pattern, in which they displayed more high-level social play than either nonsocial or low level play. Thus the predominant type of play for this group of children was high level social play. A number of these developmentally delayed children appeared to be quite animated in their play, participating in organized games such as handball or foursquare, or building in the sandbox with a peer.

TABLE 13

MEANS AND STANDARD DEVIATIONS FOR PEER INTERACTIONS
(NUMBER OF BLOCKS/TOTAL TIME)

|  |  | Autistic | Down Syndrome | Developmentally Delayed |
|---|---|---|---|---|
| Number |  | 39 | 56 | 25 |
| Play Level | Nonsocial | .58 (.30) | .33 (.27) | .31 (.22) |
|  | Low Level | .21 (.24) | .29 (.25) | .20 (.20) |
|  | High Level | .20 (.30) | .35 (.25) | .48 (.28) |
|  | Social-positive | .05 (.09) | .10 (.09) | .15 (.12) |

In contrast to the general impression that children with Down syndrome are exceedingly social, the children with Down syndrome did not seem to favor one type of play over another. This group of children was as likely to be engaged in an organized game with their peers as they were to be isolated from others during the recess period. It is interesting to note, however, that although the children with developmental delay were most likely to be engaged in high level social play, there were no differences in the proportion of high level play between the developmentally delayed and the Down syndrome groups.

### Social Play With Positive Affect

As would be expected, there also were group differences in high level play that co-occurred with positive affect, $F(2,117) = 7.91$, $p < .0006$. A Newman-Keuls test showed that all three participants groups had significantly different proportions of social positive play; autistic group less than Down syndrome group, $p < .05$, autistic group less than developmentally delayed group, $p < .0002$, Down syndrome group less than developmentally delayed group, $p < .03$ (see Table 13).

### Social Initiations

Children who spend most of the time alone must make and/or receive very few invitations for social exchange. Analyses revealed that the children with autism made fewer social bids to their peers than did the other two groups, $F(2,117) = 11.17$, $p < .0001$; autism group less than Down syndrome group, $p < .0009$, autism group less than developmentally delayed group, $p < .0001$ (see Figure 10). This must be due to the fact that far fewer children with autism made any social bids (which is discussed in more detail below) as there were no significant group differences when the number of initiations was compared including only children who made bids and covarying out language age. There were no differences between the children with Down syndrome and the children with developmental delays, so the prediction that the children with Down syndrome would be especially social was not supported. The mean, standard deviation, and range for the number of initiations of those children who initiated bids is $M = 3.3\%$, $SD = 2.4\%$, and range = 1%–13%. Overall, the children made very few bids for social interaction. The extent to which all the developmentally disabled children initiated fewer social bids than would be expected for typically developing children is unclear since no group of typically developing children was studied.

A very important finding is that there were no differences among groups with respect to the proportion of peer-made social bids. Thus, although the children with autism were less likely to reach out to others, peers were as likely to initiate social interaction with children with autism as they were with children with Down syndrome or children with developmental delays.

### Responses to Social Initiations

Play initiations are just part of the story as reception of these social bids is critical to social involvement. In question was whether social overtures were welcomed by the targeted playmate. As mentioned earlier, the prediction was that the children with autism would be less likely to accept the social

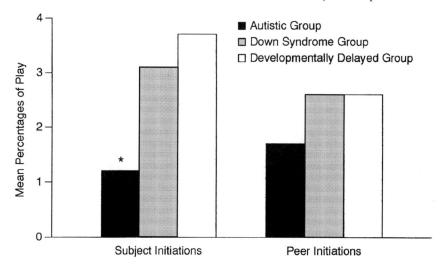

FIGURE 10.—Mean percentages of child and peer play initiations. *Indicates that the children with autism initiated peer involvement significantly less than all the other groups.

bids made by their peers. Whether the children with autism would be rejected by their peers seemed less clear.

For these analyses, percentage scores were used to take into account the baseline differences in number of play initiations. The number of accepted subject-initiations was divided by the total number of subject-initiations and the number of accepted peer-initiations were divided by the total number of peer-initiations. Because some of the participants did not have any play-initiations, data were unavailable for a number of participants. This loss of participants is telling because the numbers were not equivalent across the three groups. For subject-initiations, 18 participants with autism made no initiations, compared with 6 children with Down syndrome and none of the children with developmental delays. For peer-initiations, 11 of the children with autism never received a social bid, compared with 5 of the children with Down syndrome and 2 of the children with developmental delays. Thus, the group with autism was remarkable in terms of the number of children who did not make or receive social bids; nearly half of the participants with autism did not initiate an interaction with their peers even once.

Although there were no differences in language age for the autistic children who made or received social bids and those who did not, there were differences in language age between the three diagnostic groups when only children who made or received bids were considered. For this reason, language age was covaried in the ANOVAs. The results showed no group difference in the percentage of social bids that were accepted by peers (see Figure 11). Thus, children with autism who made social bids were just as likely to have their bids accepted as children in the other groups. For the group as a whole, only 23% of bids were rejected. In contrast, the children with autism were less likely to accept bids from their peers than the other two groups, $F(2,95) = 12.98$, $p < .00001$, adjusted mean = 41% for the children with autism, adjusted mean = 73% for the children with Down syndrome, and adjusted mean = 83% for the children with developmental delays; autism group less than Down syndrome group, $p < .0002$, autism group less than developmentally delayed group, $p < .0001$.

In summary, the social isolation of the autistic children was due more to their own behavior than that of their peers. Analyses of the proportion of the social bids to peers demonstrated that, in general, children with autism did not reach out as much to their peers or accept as many invitations as the children with Down syndrome and the children with developmental delays. Not discouraged by the paucity of invitations, peers made as many bids to the children with autism as to the other two groups and accepted as many bids from the children with autism as the other two groups.

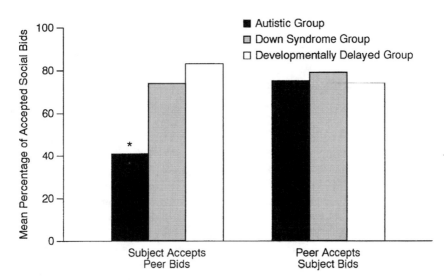

FIGURE 11.—Mean percentages of child and peer play initiations that were accepted by the other child. *Indicates that the children with autism accepted significantly fewer peer initiations than the other groups.

*Maintenance of Social Interactions*

As mentioned earlier, it was not logical simply to examine differences in the proportion of subject-initiations and peer-initiations for the groups independently of the duration of sustained high level interaction that followed the bid for social interaction. Interestingly, analyses of the average string length of high level social behaviors after a social bid by either the subject or the peer did not reveal any group differences. Children with autism, Down syndrome, or developmental delay all displayed strings of a similar length following subject or peer initiation of social interaction. Each initiation was followed by high level social play that lasted for a mean duration in 15-s blocks of about 5.72 blocks with a standard deviation of 4.71 blocks. It is also notable that there were no differences in whether the string was initiated by either the subject or the peer. These findings are compelling in that they suggest that despite differences in the number of subject-initiations and accepted entries, the children with autism can maintain an interaction as well as the children in the other two groups.

The findings support the view that social isolation is not due to the autistic child being either rejected or shunned by schoolmates or an impairment in the ability to maintain an ongoing interaction, compared to the other two diagnostic groups. Clearly, one area to focus intervention for the children with autism would be on increasing initiations of play with a partner.

## Social Activities

The proportions of the specific activities (agonistic acts and responses, responses to distress in others, rough and tumble play, affection, play organizing and sharing) were quite low and did not differ among groups. Agonistic acts, affection, and rough and tumble play occurred for a mean of 1% of the 15-s blocks for the group as a whole; the other behaviors occurred even less frequently. For the groups separately, only the developmentally delayed children engaged in agonistic acts as much as 1% of the 15-s blocks and this group and the children with Down syndrome were affectionate or involved in rough and tumble play for as much as 1% of the 15-s blocks. Thus, contrary to popular stereotypes, the autistic children were not involved in many agonistic acts and the children with Down syndrome were not very affectionate to their peers, at least on the school playground. It may also be the case that the playground is not the best place to observe these types of behaviors. Teacher aides supervise the playgrounds, and on most school grounds rough and tumble play (such as wrestling, pretend karate) are forbidden types of interaction. By and large, the adult presence may serve to discourage acts of aggression, and in some cases, demonstrations of affection.

## Vocalizations

The proportions of monologues and conversations were submitted to a repeated measures ANOVA and revealed a Group × Type of Vocalization Interaction, $F(2,117) = 9.578$, $p < .0001$. Simple main effects analyses revealed that the children with Down syndrome and the children with developmental delays engaged in significantly more conversations than the children with autism, $F(2, 117) = 9.217$, $p < .0002$. The groups did not differ significantly in the frequency of monologues. There were no differences in the proportion of monologues and conversations for the children with autism, whereas the other two groups conversed more than three times as often as they engaged in monologues.

## Interactions With Adults

The role of the adults on the playground or in the other unstructured situations did not vary for the three groups. There were no group differences in the proportions of adult initiations to the children or in adult responses to the initiations of the child. The repeated measures ANOVA showed a main effect of the direction of the adult interaction, $F(1,117) = 8.082$, $p < .0054$. The means revealed that adults were more likely to initiate interaction with the children ($M = 6\%$) than were the children likely to initiate interactions with the adults ($M = 3\%$). The adult initiations consisted of greetings, game playing and, at times, assistance in integrating a child into an activity, or breaking up a fight/argument. Whereas adults initiated interactions with children much more than participants or peers initiated with each other (5–6% versus 1–4%), the adults were mostly uninvolved with the children during the unstructured time. Frequencies of adult initiations were not significantly correlated with the amount of high level social engagement for the children in any group.

*Peer Popularity*

As discussed in the methods section, teachers filled out a questionnaire with 17 Likert scale-questions that were concerned with the child's popularity with respect to his or her classmates. A total score was made from these ratings (the higher the score, the less popular the child). Thus, 38 children with autism, 52 children with Down syndrome, and 24 children with developmental delays (still excluding the four participants with the highest language ages in this group) were studied with respect to their teacher rating of peer popularity. The teacher ratings of popularity were examined to determine whether the teachers saw one group of children as more popular than another.

Teachers tended to rate older autistic children as less popular than younger autistic children, $r(36) = -.45, p < .005$. For this reason, the ANOVA comparing the popularity of the three groups was calculated with chronological age covaried. Using a significance level of $p < .01$, the analysis did not demonstrate group differences in teacher-rated popularity. With a higher rating referring to less popularity, the respective adjusted means were as follows: autistic group = 65.73; Down syndrome group = 60.60; developmentally delayed group = 54.99.

Teachers also were asked if the children had a best friend or a group of friends. A chi-square analysis revealed that the three diagnostic groups were different with respect to the presence or absence of a best friend, $\chi^2(2) = 10.13, p < .0063$. The children with Down syndrome were the most likely to have a best friend at 64%, whereas the children with autism were the least likely to have a best friend, at 27%. The developmentally delayed group fell in the middle range, with 41% of the children's teachers reporting that the children had a best friend. There were no group differences on the teachers' ratings of whether or not the child had a group of friends. It is interesting to note that although the children with Down syndrome did not distinguish themselves with a high proportion of social play, they seemed more able to form friendships than the other children.

## DIFFERENCES IN PEER INTERACTIONS IN RELATION TO SCHOOL PLACEMENT

The social world of these children does not necessarily facilitate the development of peer interaction. Children with developmental delays are often placed in special education classrooms in which their peers experience similar difficulties in establishing social relations. When the majority of children in the classroom display difficulties in their peer interactions, there are few opportunities to observe appropriate role models. Guralnick and Groom (1985) and Strain (1984) found that children with mild developmental delays tended to be involved in more peer exchanges when they participated in integrated versus specialized settings. The quality and frequency of positive social exchanges improved when children with mild developmental delays played with CA-matched, normal children (Guralnick & Groom, 1987). The researchers hypothesized that the improvements were due to the active role taken by the normal children in organizing and involving the delayed children in meaningful social interactions. Children with autism also seem to benefit from interacting with typically developing peers (Lord & Hopkins, 1986).

Although these research findings have been used to support mainstreaming, integrated classrooms can have their own disadvantages for the development of peer interactions. First, the normal children may adopt a nurturing/maternal role toward the developmentally delayed child rather than a more balanced peer relationship. Second, if the child is fully included in a classroom of typically developing peers, the child with the developmental disability may be ostracized and/or excluded by his or her peers. An important question, then, is whether social engagement was greater for children who spent part of their school day in contact with typically developing children in contrast to children whose interactions were restricted to developmentally disabled peers.

As the children who participated in our study had a wide range of abilities, their placement in classrooms varied. Some of the children were in classrooms that included typically developing children at least some of the time, whereas others were in classrooms that never included typically developing children. The percentages are shown in Table 14. Analyses revealed that the differences in the number of children in each diagnostic group who were in special education versus full inclusion or a mixed setting were not significant, $\chi^2(2) = 3.48, p < .18$.

We also compared the number of children in each group who had access to typically developing children on the playground. Children were considered to have access to typically developing children if (1) they were in a regular class and there were no other children with obvious developmental disorders available during recess, (2) the child shared the recess period with children from both special and regular education classes, or (3) the child was

TABLE 14

PERCENTAGE OF CHILDREN WITH ACCESS TO TYPICALLY DEVELOPING
CHILDREN IN THE CLASSROOM OR ON THE PLAYGROUND

|  | Classroom | Playground |
|---|---|---|
| Autistic Group | 43% | 54% |
| Down Syndrome Group | 38% | 61% |
| Developmentally Delayed Group | 62% | 69% |

observed in both a special education only and a mixed setting (e.g., the child ate lunch with his or her special education classmates and then went out to a playground that had both regular education and special education students). If the child shared the recess period with children from both special and regular education classes but there were no regular education students in proximity to him or her on the playground, then the child was considered not to have access to typically developing children for the purposes of the present study. The percentages of children who had access to typically developing children are shown in Table 14. The three diagnostic groups also did not differ significantly in terms of the proportions of children who had access to typically developing children during recess, $\chi^2(2) = 4.14$, $p < .13$. Since the children in the three groups did not differ in their access to typically developing children, the differences in the peer interactions of the children with autism cannot be attributed to variations in the availability of typically developing peers.

In order to investigate whether peer interaction varied as a function of access to typically developing children, comparisons were made of the peer interactions of children who had access to typically developing children (labeled as Special Education in Figure 12) and those who did not (labeled as Mixed or Full Inclusion in Figure 12). Separate repeated measures, 2 (Access to typically developing children) × 3 (Play Level), ANOVAs were calculated for each of the three diagnostic groups. As language ages differed for children with access to typically developing children and those without such access, language age was included as a covariate in the analyses. There was a significant interaction between Access to Typically Developing Children and Levels of Play for the children with autism, $F(2,72) = 9.36$, $p < .0002$. Simple main effects demonstrated that the autistic children with exposure to typically developing children on the playground, in contrast to those without such exposure, were engaged in more high level interaction, $F(1,35) = 4.72$, $p < .04$, and less nonsocial play, $F(1,35) = 9.56$, $p < .004$, even with statistical control for differences in language abilities. Levels of peer engagement did not vary across playground experiences for the children with Down

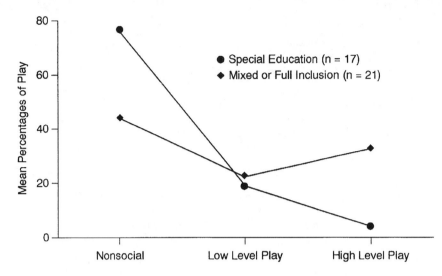

FIGURE 12.—Mean percentages of levels of play. The children with autism who had access to typically developing peers were involved in nonsocial activities for a greater proportion of time and in high level peer engagement for a smaller proportion of time than the children with autism who did not have access to typically developing peers on the playground.

syndrome and the children with developmental delays. It should be noted that only eight children with developmental delays were on playgrounds without typically developing children. In summary, these results show that autistic children with access to typically developing peers were more socially engaged than children without such access.

Because the causes of this greater sociability are unknown, it seemed worthwhile to determine if the children or their peers acted differently on playgrounds that included typically developing children. The proportion of time blocks in which autistic children and their peers initiated interactions did not vary as a function of their access to typically developing children nor were there differences in the rates of peer initiation or of acceptance of bids by either the autistic children or their peers.

## DISCUSSION

There are several limitations in this study that make interpretation of the results somewhat difficult. First, a group of typically developing children of the same level of functioning was not studied so that no comparisons can be made of the social engagement and behaviors of these developmentally disabled children with typically developing children. As discussed in the introduction to this monograph, typically developing children with similar language abilities are likely to be in a very different school environment making comparisons difficult. A second limitation is that the identity of the peers was not recorded so that there is no way to determine whether the subject initiated interactions with the same child repeatedly or with different children. Similarly, the diagnosis of peers was not established or recorded so that there is no way to tell whether children with the same diagnosis chose each other for social interactions or whether peer interactions involved children from different diagnostic groups. Given rules about confidentiality, there was no way that information about the identity of the peers, no less their diagnoses, could have been recorded without obtaining consent from the parents of all the children in every class in all the schools. Moreover, establishing the diagnoses of the peers would be no small task and would have been impossible in this investigation. In the future, laboratory studies of peer interaction are needed as this is the only way to assess and diagnose all the children involved in a standardized way. Even a small classroom study probably would not work because the language abilities of the children are not likely to be matched. A laboratory study also could include typically developing children observed in the same setting as the developmentally disabled children.

Despite these limitations, the data collected at school provide an interesting portrait of peer relations for the children in our study. By and large, the hypotheses about the social life of children with autism were supported. The children with autism tended to play in isolation from others and were less interactive overall. As predicted, children with autism initiated social interaction and accepted the overtures of others less frequently than other children. Although somewhat fewer autistic children were invited into play, social bids to those invited were as frequent as for the other groups. Thus their peers were not shunning them any more than was true for the other groups. Moreover, for those children with autism who made bids for social engagement, their bids were accepted as much as was true for other children. Finally, children with autism were able to maintain interactions as long as the other children once these were begun. Thus, the results show a mixed picture where the children are as isolated as we had suspected but they are not rejected as much as we had feared.

One implication is that interventions should concentrate on increasing the social initiations that autistic children make on the school playground. Of course, we do not know whether increasing their interactions would also increase their rate of rejection by peers but this could be measured. As the other children both attempt to engage autistic children and are responsive to them and the children with autism maintain social engagements for as long as the other children, promoting initiations and responses of the autistic children seems to be what is needed.

The reasons why the children with autism did not accept the bids of others is not clear from these data. It would be helpful to have information about the quality of the bids that peers made to the autistic children. A previous study has shown that the quality and type of initiations affect the likelihood of positive responses of the children with autism (Lord & Hopkins, 1986). The children with autism may have been rejecting initiations that were negative or inappropriate. In future research, the nature of initiations has to be considered (see Hauck et al., 1995, for categories of initiations).

Increasing the social involvement of the children with autism may be very difficult given their social incapacities. We observed very few interventions, however, by the adults on the school playground. It seems important to attempt to improve the social life of the children with autism by helping them to enter social involvements. Perhaps special education could be refocused so that the social education that occurs on school playgrounds becomes as important as what occurs in the classroom.

The children with Down syndrome were more interactive than the children with autism but they did not differ from the other developmentally delayed children. Thus, the children with Down syndrome do not show the level of peer interaction that might have been expected from their absorbed interest in the emotional reactions of adults in the laboratory. The fact that most of the children with Down syndrome do have best friends is a significant social achievement. They may be able to form relationships that are more rare among the developmentally delayed and almost absent for the children with autism. At the same time, social skills need to be developed that allow interactions with larger groups of individuals. For this reason, adult interventions that improve peer interactions on the playground would seem to be valuable for all the developmentally disabled children studied in this project.

The characteristics of the playground environment had an association with the level of peer interactions of children with autism that was not observed with the other developmentally disabled children. Although the autistic children with access to typically developing children showed more social engagement, we were unable to identify ways in which this was mediated as the children with autism initiated and accepted social bids less than the other children in both settings.

Access to typically developing children was not related to level of peer engagement of children with Down syndrome and other developmental delays. It is very important that neither these negative results nor the positive results with autistic children be taken seriously without confirmation from studies using randomized assignment of children to school conditions. Besides the impossibility of interpreting negative results, there is a lack of randomization in the everyday assignment of children to school settings. Children are selected for certain school placements because of their characteristics. Therefore, the improved peer interactions of the autistic children with access to typically developing peers may be a function of the autistic children's abilities and characteristics rather than the school environment. Although we have covaried language abilities, there are many other child traits that may have led to their school placements that could account for the differences in social engagement. Similarly, the lack of significant effects of access to typically developing children could be a function of the characteristics of the children with Down syndrome and developmental delays who have been assigned to each setting.

# VI. CORRELATES AND PREDICTORS OF PEER INTERACTIONS IN SCHOOL

An important goal of this study is to identify the characteristics of the children that foster social involvement. Thus, this chapter examines both concurrent and predictive relations between peer interactions and other measures of child competence. Concurrent factors that are likely to influence peer interactions include the cognitive and language abilities of the children, their behaviors on the playground, and their responsiveness to the needs and emotions of others.

## CONCURRENT CORRELATES OF PEER INTERACTIONS

### Relations Between High Level Social Interactions and Children's Abilities and Behaviors

Given that social exchange requires the capacity for communication, children with more adequate cognitive and language abilities should be better able to form social relationships at school than children with less adequate cognitive and language skills. In order to examine this hypothesis with this sample, correlations were computed between mental age and language age with the proportion of time that the children were involved in high level social interactions. Mental age and language age were significantly related to high level social play for the children with autism and developmental delays but not for the children with Down syndrome (see Table 15). Children's high level peer involvement did not vary with their chronological ages. The identification of an association between cognitive abilities and peer engagement in autistic children replicates findings of Stone and Caro-Martinez (1990). Thus, as mentioned earlier in this monograph, cognitively advanced children with autism are more involved with their peers than low-functioning children with autism. The association between language age, a measure of

TABLE 15

Correlations Between High-Level Social Play With
Child Characteristics and Behaviors

| Child Characteristic and Behaviors | Autistic Group $n = 39$ | DS Group $n = 56$ | DD Group $n = 25$ |
|---|---|---|---|
| Chronological Age | −.13 | .05 | −.06 |
| Mental Age | .44** | .30 | .60*** |
| Language Age | .49** | .32 | .57** |
| Child initiates interaction | .59*** | .29 | .19 |
| Peer initiates interaction | .28 | −.01 | −.27 |
| Length that child maintains interaction | .43** | .69*** | .38 |
| Child's initiation is rejected | −.33 | −.40** | −.52** |
| Peer's initiation is rejected | −.46** | −.50** | −.21 |

**$p < .01$
***$p < .001$

communicative competence, and peer engagement, a measure of social competence, shows that these two forms of social competence are related.

The degree to which children are engaged in social interaction may depend either on their own behaviors or that of their peers. In other words, peer engagement may be associated with the child's initiation and acceptance of bids for play or with the peer's initiation and acceptance of bids. In order to evaluate the role of each partner in affecting children's social involvement, correlations were calculated between high level social play and the following behaviors: frequency that child or peer initiates social interaction, proportion of participant or peer initiated acts that are rejected, and the average length of time that the participant maintains a social engagement after it is initiated.

The frequency with which the autistic children initiated peer interactions and the length of time that initiated acts were maintained by the children with autism and the children with Down syndrome were correlated with the proportion of time that the children were involved in high level social play. The overall frequency with which peers directed social bids to the participants did not determine how much any of the children were engaged in social interaction. The extent to which the children with autism and children with Down syndrome rejected their peers' social bids was negatively associated with their social engagement. For the developmentally delayed children and the Down syndrome children, an important determinant of social engagement was the percentage of time that they were rebuffed by peers. These findings suggest that, even more than for other children, the social engagement of autistic children is a function of their own proclivity to be engaged rather than their acceptance by others.

*Peer Interactions in High-Functioning Children With Autism*

Given that social involvement is higher in cognitively able children with autism, it may be that high-functioning children with autism are able to compensate completely for their social difficulties. Evidence of compensation for deficits with social and emotional understanding have been documented in high-functioning children with autism in several studies. Alternatively, the school playground may be such a difficult place for children with autism that, even when they have good cognitive skills, these are not sufficient for them to overcome their social handicaps completely.

To address this issue, a repeated measures ANOVA on the play levels of just the children who had an IQ of 70 or over at follow-up testing was calculated. None of the children with Down syndrome had IQs over 70, so only the data from the children with autism ($n = 13$) and the children with developmental delays ($n = 12$) were examined. The high-functioning children with autism had a mean IQ of 88.2 ($SD = 14.38$), whereas the high-functioning children with developmental delays had a mean IQ of 92.9 ($SD = 16.5$) and very similar language ages. Although there was a significant main effect of play levels, $F(2,46) = 8.16$, $p < .0009$, and the Group × Play Level interaction only approached significance, $F(2,46) = 2.64$, $p < .08$, only the difference in play level for the developmentally delayed children was significant, $F(2,46) = 8.43$, $p < .0001$. The developmentally delayed children were socially engaged more than they were solitary ($M = 65\%$ vs. 22%) whereas the autistic children spent equal amounts of time in high level play and nonsocial play ($M = 41\%$ vs. 40%). Moreover, there was a trend toward a group difference between the children with autism and the developmentally delayed children in terms of high level social play, $F(1,46) = 4.70$, $p < .04$. The high-functioning developmentally delayed children were somewhat more socially engaged than the high-functioning autistic children (see Figure 13).

This trend was congruent with some of our impressions during the school observations. Some high-functioning children with autism were able to sustain quite intensive social interactions. There were a number of occasions, however, during which a high-functioning child with autism who was engaged in a high level social activity suddenly broke off with the activity and wandered off by himself. As a case in point, one high-functioning boy with autism spent the first part of his lunch recess engaged in high level pretend play with his peers, a rough and tumble game in which there were "good guy" and "bad guy" roles; suddenly, he ran off to the far end of the playground and spent the remainder of his recess by himself in the sandbox. The teacher noted that this was typical behavior for this child; he simply would reach a point during play where he "needed" to be by himself.

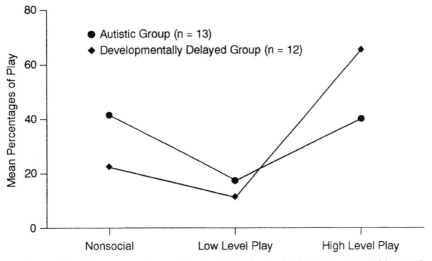

FIGURE 13.—Mean percentages of levels of play for the high-functioning children with autism and with developmental delays.

A second example was a boy who was involved in a lively handball game with his classmates. Frustrated at losing a point, he explosively stomped away from the court and shouted at the playground aide about how "unfair" the game was. His teacher mentioned that this was his modus operandi, also noting that if he scored less than 100% on his spelling tests he would become very upset. These high expectations and need for predictability seemed to be fairly typical for this group of high-functioning children.

### Peer Interactions in Children With Down Syndrome

In the previous chapter, we reported that the children with Down syndrome had a somewhat different pattern of social interaction than the children with developmental delays. The developmentally delayed group, however, included both high-functioning and low-functioning children, whereas the Down syndrome group consisted only of low-functioning children. When the proportions of the three types of play were compared in a 2 (Group) × 3 (Play Level) ANOVA only with the data from low-functioning children, there were no significant group, level of play, or interaction effects. Thus, the social engagement patterns of the children with Down syndrome were just like those of the developmentally delayed children with IQs less than 70.

*Relations Between Peer Interactions and Social Responsiveness*

One possibility is that children who are more responsive to the feelings and needs of others are more able to be involved with peers. Thus, we might expect children who showed more prosocial behaviors in interaction with the experimenter and greater responsiveness to the experimenter's distress to have higher levels of social engagement and initiation.

This is an important question from several viewpoints. First, the question is central to the issue as to how much overlap there is in different components of social competence. Second, from the viewpoint of intervention, if relations exist between components of social competence, then fostering one aspect of social competence may promote abilities in other areas. For example, increasing interaction with peers may give children greater affective knowledge through direct experience in emotionally charged situations. In line with this hypothesis, Hauck, Fein, Waterhouse, and Feinstein (1995) showed that adaptive social skills, vocabulary, functional use of language, affect matching, and emotional understanding were related to peer initiations in a sample with autism. Past research, then, suggests that other components of social competence are related to peer interaction skills.

As discussed in Chapter IV, both the prosocial behaviors and response to the experimenter's distress were observed in the laboratory shortly before the school observation. For these current analyses, two behavioral ratings of prosocial behavior were used: a mean rating of helping to clear the table and clean up the spilled juice and a mean rating of sharing the photographs and food. Response to distress was measured by the duration of looking to the experimenter's face and the ratings of concern. As language age was correlated with some of the prosocial and emotional responsiveness measures as well as with high-level social interactions, correlations were computed with and without language age covaried.

For the children with autism, both prosocial behaviors and emotional responsiveness measures were correlated with high level social play and frequency of initiations (see Table 16). Fewer measures were correlated with peer interactions when language age was covaried so that some of this stability may have been due to the variations in communicative abilities rather than social responsiveness within the autistic group. The extent to which the autistic children helped the experimenter when she was having difficulties and showed concern for her when she was distressed, however, was correlated with peer engagement and tendency to initiate interactions even when variations in communicative abilities were statistically constrained. There was only one statistically significant association for the children with Down syndrome and none for the developmentally delayed group. Because the tendency to read the cues of others and respond to these cues is so limited

TABLE 16

CORRELATIONS BETWEEN PEER INTERACTIONS WITH PROSOCIAL AND RESPONSIVE BEHAVIORS

| | Autistic Group $n = 37$ | | DS Group $n = 40$ | | DD Group $n = 19$ | |
|---|---|---|---|---|---|---|
| | Social Play | Initiates | Social Play | Initiates | Social Play | Initiates |
| Helps | .48**[a] | .53***[a] | .33** | .19 | .16 | .19 |
| Shares | .49** | .35 | .18 | .28 | .17 | −.04 |
| Looks to Distressed E | .33 | .22 | .13 | .13 | .15 | .29 |
| Concern for Distressed E | .20 | .46**[a] | .06 | .06 | .23 | .35 |

[a]Remains significant when language age covaried.
**$p < .01$
***$p < .001$

within the autistic group, this tendency may be particularly powerful when it is manifested by children with autism.

## EARLY PREDICTORS OF CHILDHOOD PEER INTERACTION

### Prediction of Peer Interactions From Communicative and Play Behaviors in Early Childhood

The second goal of this chapter was to determine the extent to which the children's early communicative and representation play skills predicted to their peer interactions in childhood. If these early skills are precursors to later peer social competence, this would argue for the importance of fostering these early skills. In Chapter III, we showed that autistic children with better nonverbal communication skills made greater gains in expressive language over the period from early to later childhood. Nonverbal communication skills would seem to be as important for peer play as for language acquisition. For this reason, the associations between nonverbal communication skills and play behaviors with the proportion of time that children were involved in high level peer play and the frequency of initiations were examined.

### Preliminary Analyses

Given the stability over time in the children's mental and verbal abilities shown in Chapters II and III, early mental and verbal abilities might predict later peer involvement. For this reason, correlations were computed for each group between high-level social play and number of initiations with early childhood mental age, language age, and DQ. Number of initiations was not predicted by earlier mental or verbal abilities for the children with autism or Down syndrome. Autistic children who were more intelligent when tested in the preschool period, however, were more socially engaged later in childhood, $r(36) = .44$, $p < .006$. For this reason, subsequent associations were examined both with and without early intelligence as a covariate.

### Nonverbal Communication in Early Childhood and Peer Interaction

The results showed that some nonverbal communication skills were predictive of social engagement for the children with autism (see Table 17). When preschool DQ was covaried, the children with autism who initiated joint attention more often were more socially engaged with peers in midchildhood than children who had initiated joint attention less. Similarly, children with autism who responded to the social bids of the experimenter in early childhood were more likely to be engaged with peers later in childhood, although this was not independent of previous intelligence level. There also was some continuity for the children with Down syndrome. Children with Down syndrome who initiated social interaction more with the experimenter when they were preschool age made more social initiations with

TABLE 17

CORRELATIONS BETWEEN COMMUNICATION ACTS IN EARLY CHILDHOOD
AND PEER INTERACTIONS IN LATER CHILDHOOD

| | Autistic Group $n = 34$ | | DS Group $n = 50$ | | DD Group $n = 25$ | |
|---|---|---|---|---|---|---|
| | Social Play | Initiates | Social Play | Initiates | Social Play | Initiates |
| Initiates Joint Attention | .50**[a] | .32 | .25 | .30 | .25 | .13 |
| Initiates Behavior Regulation | .31 | .20 | −.04 | .11 | .23 | .08 |
| Initiates Social Interaction | .22 | .24 | .18 | .56*** | .08 | .07 |
| Responds to Joint Attention | .35 | −.04 | .24 | .33 | .10 | .21 |
| Responds to Social Interaction | .42** | .36 | .02 | −.12 | .35 | .04 |

[a]Remains significant when intake IQ covaried.
**$p < .01$
***$p < .001$

94

peers when they were school-age. There were no significant predictions for the children with developmental delays.

*Representational Play in Early Childhood and Peer Interaction*

A similar analysis was carried out of the correlations between play behaviors and peer interaction variables (see Table 18). The number of functional and symbolic play acts used by the children with autism when they were between 3 and 5 years old predicted social engagment in the mid-school years. There were no other significant correlations although there is a trend toward an association ($p < .05$) between the number of different functional play acts and the frequency of social bids on the playground for the other two groups. We have argued previously that representational play requires not only some symbolic understanding but also social observation and engagement. Children almost always reproduce social acts in play or, at least, actions that they have observed others perform. Thus, young children with developmental disabilities who act out a variety of functional play scenarios may be somewhat more aware of the actions of others and more likely to involve others in their play. The continuity between representational play in early childhood and peer initiation and engagement in childhood may stem from an underlying link involving social awareness that both types of activities require.

A hierarchical regression was calculated in order to determine which of the early behaviors best predicted the autistic children's high level social engagement with peers. Initial DQ, the frequency of initiating joint attention, and the number of different functional play acts were entered into the regression in that order. As can be seen from Table 19, the three early characteristics of the children accounted for 39% of the variance in their social engagement at follow-up. When the order of entry of variables was reversed, the frequency of initiating joint attention did not enter into the

TABLE 18

CORRELATIONS BETWEEN PLAY BEHAVIOR IN EARLY CHILDHOOD AND
PEER INTERACTION IN LATER CHILDHOOD

| Number of Play Acts | Autistic Group $n = 39$ | | DS Group $n = 31$ | | DD Group $n = 25$ | |
|---|---|---|---|---|---|---|
| | Social Play | Initiates | Social Play | Initiates | Social Play | Initiates |
| Functional Play | .45**[a] | .36 | −.08 | .38 | .28 | .43 |
| Symbolic Play | .39** | .02 | −.15 | .38 | .28 | .08 |

[a]Remains significant when intake IQ covaried.
**$p < .01$

TABLE 19

Hierarchical Regressions Between Preschool Behaviors and
High Level Social Play for the Autistic Sample at Follow-up

| Variable | $R^2$ Change | F | $p <$ |
|---|---|---|---|
| IQ | .20 | 11.10 | .002 |
| Initiates Joint Attention | .10 | 5.37 | .03 |
| Different Functional Play Acts | .15 | 8.10 | .007 |
| Adjusted $R^2$ | .39 | 8.19 | .0001 |

regression once the frequency of different functional play acts had been considered.

## DISCUSSION

Both concurrent and earlier characteristics of the children were associated with their level of peer involvement. Children with better cognitive and language abilities were more involved with peers. This could be because they were better equipped to communicate with their peers but it may also be that peer engagement enhances cognitive and language development. Peer play appears to have an important educational function not only for human children but for other primates as well. A vicious cycle may emerge in which a socially incompetent child has little interaction with peers, limiting opportunities for further development of social comprehension.

Better cognitive and language skills improved the peer competence of the children with autism but some of their social limitations still remained. Unlike the high-functioning children with developmental delays, the high-functioning children with autism did not prefer to be engaged in high level play and spent an equivalent percentage of time in solitary activities. This may be because of a basic need to be alone or because social interactions are so taxing for them that they can tolerate only so much social involvement. One limitation of this sample is that very few of the children are very high-functioning. More cognitively competent autistic children may show higher levels of social involvement than is true for this group.

The findings of this study suggest that communicative abilities and social responsiveness are important characteristics that shape peer involvement. Relating to peers on an emotional level and engaging in behaviors such as sharing and helping may lead the child with autism to be a more desirable playmate. In addition, the ability to understand the needs of others as manifested in prosocial behavior may make social interactions more comprehensible to these autistic children so that peer engagements are more pleasurable. Thus, these results suggest that educating autistic children about the reactions of others so that they can learn to make appropriate social responses may be one avenue to facilitating their peer relationships.

The other pathway to improved social competence may be through the child's early social and representational abilities. The capacity for nonverbal communication and for representational play predicted to the level of social engagement of the children with autism. It would seem worthwhile to attempt to identify factors that improve nonverbal communication and play abilities in young children with autism as a way to further their overall social competence.

# VII. SUMMARY AND DISCUSSION

This chapter begins with a discussion of the findings for each group of children framed in terms of the goals outlined in the introductory chapter. Limitations of the study are discussed as are clinical implications and areas for future investigation.

## CHILDREN WITH AUTISM

The first goal of the study was to determine the extent to which there was continuity and change in diagnosis, level of intelligence, and language skills. The results showed that all the children with autism continued to have severe problems in the areas of social and language development. Nearly all the children with autism continued to manifest a sufficient number of symptoms to meet all the diagnostic criteria for autism. In contrast to this continuity in diagnosis, measured intelligence changed a great deal for many of the children with autism. Intelligence test scores increased in about half the sample of children with autism, with increases averaging about 22 points. These increases were large enough so that 11 children with autism who originally were functioning in the mentally retarded range could no longer be considered mentally retarded at follow-up. Declines in intelligence also were sizeable, averaging 23 IQ points across all the diagnostic groups. For the autistic group considered as a whole, intelligence remained stable, with DQ/IQs changing from 51 at intake to 49 at follow-up. Thus, there was considerable group stability but marked individual discontinuity in intelligence over time.

As a group, the children with autism made very little progress in their language skills over time. They started with a mean language age of 18 months and had a mean language age of only 46 months some 8–9 years later. However, individual children were able to change much more than this. Only 1 of the 11 children with autism who moved out of the mentally retarded group started this study with receptive language capacities over 23 months at initial testing but all wound up with receptive language ages equivalent to 6–9 years olds. The gain in language age for these 11 children was much greater, $M = 66.1$ months, $SD = 18.4$, than for the children who remained mentally retarded, $M = 10.7$ months, $SD = 7.3$, $t(11.4) = 9.67$, $p < .0001$. Thus, it can be said that discontinuity in intelligence is manifested in the acquisition of receptive and expressive language skills, although this is not meant to imply any direction of effects.

The second goal of the follow-up was to reexamine the data using the larger sample to determine whether the previously identified deficits in social communication, representational play, and emotional responsiveness were still evident. For the most part, the analyses of the larger database confirmed the previous findings. The deficit in initiating joint attention and responding to joint attention was clear. The children with autism also showed somewhat less requesting behaviors than the children with developmental delays, a small difference that required the larger database to be evident, and remained significant at follow-up. In addition, at follow-up, the children with autism remained deficient in the frequency with which they initiated both joint attention and behavior regulation. Moreover, there was continuity from intake to follow-up in the extent to which children with autism initiated joint attention.

As in the studies with smaller samples, children with autism showed less functional and symbolic play. With language age statistically controlled, the children with autism demonstrated a smaller number of functional play acts than the children with Down syndrome and the typically developing children and a smaller number of symbolic play acts than all the other groups.

In terms of responsiveness to the distress of others, the reanalysis of the larger database confirmed that the children with autism attended less to the distressed adult than the other groups and showed less interest and concern for the distressed adult than the typically developing children and the children with developmental delays. Moreover, this pattern of results was maintained over time in that the children with autism continued to look less at the face of a distressed adult and appeared less concerned than the other developmentally disabled children. Judging by the results from the investigation of response to anger, this pattern is not due to an inability by the children with autism to differentiate between affects or a tendency to avoid attending to strong affect. The children with autism were not as attentive to the experimenter's face as the other children in either the neutral or angry condition but they differentiated between the two emotions in terms of their behavioral responses. Anger seemed to be particularly potent for the children with autism in that it drew their attention more than neutral facial expressions and there were no group differences in interest or concern when the experimenter pretended to be angry.

A third goal of the follow-up study was to compare the social competence of the school-age children with autism with the social competence of the other developmentally disabled children. We had originally intended to measure social competence in four ways, in terms of communicative abilities, social understanding, prosocial behaviors, and peer interactions. Only about one third of the sample of children with autism, however, were verbally skillful enough at follow-up to respond to questions about their social understanding (a point that should be kept in mind in reference to studies of social comprehension and Theory of Mind in children with autism.) For this reason, we have concentrated on communicative abilities, prosocial behavior, and peer interactions. In line with our predictions, children with autism were rated as less cooperative and less sharing during a social interaction situation with the experimenter. They were also less involved in interactive social play with peers and less likely to initiate and respond to social bids, although they maintained social interactions for as long once these had been initiated and were not rebuffed by their peers more than was true for the other children. Teachers rated the children with autism as less likely to have a best friend than the other groups of children. Overall, then, the children with autism continued in the mid-elementary school years to be less socially interactive and responsive than other developmentally disabled children.

Related to the previous goal, we also aimed to describe the associations between cognitive and language abilities and social competence as well as the relations among the various forms of social competence in each diagnostic group. The results showed that cognitively and verbally skillful children were more socially engaged with their peers. Those children with autism who engaged in more prosocial behavior with the experimenter in the laboratory and expressed more concern about the distressed experimenter were more likely to initiate social interactions with their peers in school and were somewhat more engaged on the playground. Thus, for the children with autism, there were links between cognitive and language abilities, social responsiveness, and peer engagement. Peer engagement also varied with the nature of the playground milieu but the causes of this variation were not identified in this study.

The final aim was to determine whether nonverbal communication and representational play skills were predictors of the language acquisition and peer engagement of children with autism. In line with previous findings using smaller samples, the results demonstrated that children with autism who initiated joint attention, responded to joint attention, and used a greater diversity of functional and symbolic play acts were concurrently more verbally adept. Moreover, autistic children who engaged in more nonverbal communication acts of all kinds gained more verbal expressive abilities over the course of a year. Long-term gains in expressive language were predicted by the extent to which children with autism responded to others' bids for joint attention and the diversity of functional play acts. Responsiveness to joint attention seemed to carry more weight than the diversity of functional play in this prediction.

The extent to which the autistic children initiated social interaction and were engaged with peers was predicted by their developmental quotient at intake as well as some of their nonverbal communication and play behaviors. When initial developmental quotient was constrained, the frequency of initiating joint attention and the diversity of functional play acts predicted social engagement. Thus, as shown in Tables 17–19, the results confirmed the hypothesis that nonverbal communication and symbolic play skills would be predictors of subsequent verbal and social competence, and that these predictions would be independent of initial developmental abilities.

## CHILDREN WITH DOWN SYNDROME

The pattern of continuity in intelligence and language skills was very different for the children with Down syndrome compared to those in the other groups. The children with Down syndrome were the only group to show a significant decline in intelligence. This decline was 20 points from the first to the third testing and 16.6 points from the second to the third testing, when they were same ages as the children with developmental delays, whose decline of 2 points was significantly less. In terms of individual change, only 3 of the 34 children with Down syndrome showed increases in intelligence test scores in contrast to 22 of the 43 children with autism and 14 of 32 children with developmental delays. Moreover, the size of the increase was very small, averaging only about 5 points in contrast to 22 points for the children with autism and 17 points for the children with developmental delays. While 40 of the children with Down syndrome did not test in the mentally retarded range at intake and 30 did not at the first follow-up, all the children had IQs less than 70 at follow-up.

Patterns of continuity and change were also different in language skills. The children with autism and Down syndrome did not differ from each other in the extent of change in their language ages (28 months and 23 months respectively) but the children with developmental delays gained more (36 months) over a comparable period. The biggest difference between groups was in the relation of expressive language to receptive language. The two were comparable for the children with autism at both time periods and for the developmentally delayed children at follow-up, but receptive language was higher than expressive language at both time points for the children with Down syndrome. Moreover, there was no group stability in expressive language for the children with Down syndrome whereas there was for receptive language for this group and for both receptive and expressive language for the other groups.

Although the children with Down syndrome appeared to be specifically impaired in language abilities, this was not true for their nonverbal communication, play skills, empathic responsiveness, prosocial behavior, or peer engagement. The expanded database showed that all the children with developmental disabilities requested objects or assistance less than the typically developing children, thereby failing to support our earlier conclusion with a smaller sample that this difference was only true for children with Down syndrome. Moreover, at follow-up the children with Down syndrome did not differ from the developmentally delayed children in the frequency with which they initiated requests. Not only did the children with Down syndrome show equivalent nonverbal communication and play skills but some of their play appeared to be even a bit better than that of the typically developing children. In terms of empathic responsiveness to others, they were comparable to the developmentally delayed groups except that they showed somewhat less interest and concern for a distressed adult at intake but this was not true at follow-up. The frequency of prosocial behaviors in the laboratory and social behaviors at school were comparable for the children with Down syndrome and those with developmental delays. There were no significant associations between cognitive skills and prosocial behaviors in the laboratory with peer engagement on the playground.

The hypothesis that nonverbal communication and play skills would be correlated with language abilities was confirmed. Children with Down syndrome who initiated joint attention and responded to bids for joint attention were more verbally adept. Similarly, play behaviors were concurrently associated with language abilities. The amount of variance in language abilities accounted for by nonverbal communication and play skills was smaller for the children with Down syndrome than for the children with autism and developmental delays.

Representational play skills did not predict either short-term or long-term gain in expressive language abilities or level of peer engagement for the children with Down syndrome, although there was a trend for children who showed more early representational play to initiate peer interactions later. The capacity to initiate social interactions seemed to be the strongest predictor of later development in that the extent to which the child with Down syndrome initiated social interactions during the administration of the ESCS was predictive of short-term and long-term gain in expressive language skills and of the frequency that the child initiated social bids on the school playground. Whereas the proclivity to initiate social interactions seemed particularly stable and predictive for the children with Down syndrome, this was not true for social responsiveness during the administration of the ESCS, which either did not predict or was even negatively related to later outcomes.

These results address an important question regarding the extent to which the social proclivities of the children with Down syndrome are advantageous for their later development. While it might be thought that the social involvement of the young Down syndrome child comes at a cost, in fact, the tendency to initiate social interactions with the experimenter is a strong predictor of the tendency to initiate social interactions with peers. While long durations of attention to the faces of others seems to characterize more slowly developing children with Down syndrome and does not confer any advantage over time, the ability to initiate social engagement does seem to be stable and to facilitate peer involvement at school.

Problems in the development of language skills among children with Down syndrome cannot be traced to early deficits in representation and communication. The identification of a problem in auditory memory among children with Down syndrome that seems tied to difficulties in language acquisition (Fowler, 1995; Wang & Bellugi, 1994) provides a better lead for intervention.

## CHILDREN WITH DEVELOPMENTAL DELAYS

The children with developmental delays were included in this study as a heterogeneous contrast group who could be matched with the other two groups on chronological, mental, and language ages. Sometimes, this matching required that the data from the most intelligent and verbally skillful children be excluded from the comparisons. Overall, the developmentally delayed children showed patterns of behavior that were more similar to those of the children with Down syndrome and the typically developing children than the children with autism. This was true for nonverbal communication, social responsiveness, prosocial behavior, and peer interaction. The developmentally delayed children did not show the strengths in representational play or the weaknesses in expressive language demonstrated by the children with Down syndrome. Whereas the concurrent associations between nonverbal communication, play, and language were similar for the three groups, the predictive relations often were smaller for the developmentally delayed group than for either of the other groups, most likely because the developmentally delayed group was much smaller. Because of the size of this sample and its heterogeneity, few overall conclusions can be drawn from this study about children with developmental delays.

## A RECONSIDERATION OF CHARACTERISTIC DEFICITS

In the first chapter of this monograph, three criteria (specificity, universality, and uniqueness) for determining that a deficit is central to a particular syndrome were described. The results of this study suggest that autistic children have central deficits in initiating joint attention, attending to the affect of others, and symbolic play that are specific, universal, and unique. Using the same criteria, children with Down syndrome appear to have language deficits that are specific and universal if not unique. The criteria of specificity and universality have been addressed more effectively in this monograph than in our previous studies because of the variety of measures examined and the extensive follow-up. We also made progress in addressing the issue of uniqueness to some extent. When we compared children with Down syndrome to children with other developmental disorders in this monograph, the requesting deficit no longer appeared unique to children with Down syndrome as it had without that comparison. Some of the deficits that appear unique to children with autism, however, also may characterize other groups of children, such as nonautistic children with Fragile X syndrome. For this reason, the uniqueness criteria may rarely be satisfied. Furthermore, uniqueness of deficits may be better conceptualized in terms of the magnitude of group differences as well as in terms of organized patterns of deficits, rather than specific deficiencies, to capture precise distinctions between syndromes.

## INDIVIDUAL CHARACTERISTICS VERSUS GROUP DIFFERENCES

The identification of group differences is often less compelling for parents, teachers, and clinicians than it is for researchers. The major clinical value of knowing about group differences is that individuals responsible for a child can be reassured that certain characteristics of the child are due to his disorder. At the same time, this kind of reassurance is not always useful, as the responsible adults still have to deal with the characteristic, no matter what its cause. For example, although mental retardation is not a defining characteristic of autism, parents with mentally retarded autistic children have to plan different activities for their children than parents whose children are autistic but not mentally retarded. This difference in outlook needs to be kept in mind when researchers attempt to communicate with parents, teachers, and clinicians.

## GROUP STABILITY AND INDIVIDUAL CHANGE

The investigation of continuity and change involves several difficulties. One difficulty is that the characterization of continuity and change varies as a function of the method used. For example, in this monograph, we have used three different ways of describing changes in intelligence scores, each of which has its advantages and disadvantages. One way is to show group changes. Groups may remain stable, however, whereas individuals within the group show considerable discontinuity. This pattern or results is demonstrated dramatically by the group stability in intelligence scores of the children with autism, whereas individual children show massive gains and losses in intelligence scores. Another method is to use the accepted cutoff for mental retardation and evaluate changes around that cutoff, a method that has the advantage of using a differentiation that guides decisions about school placement and provision of services but that equates the intelligence scores of a child with a 60 IQ and a child with a 15 IQ. A third way is to describe the number of children who increase or decrease in intelligence scores and the mean level of increase and decrease. This method operates, however, as if every point change in intelligence score had equivalent functional consequences.

Descriptions of change and continuity in intelligence scores are simple in some ways in comparison to change and continuity in behavior. This is true because almost every behavioral measure has to be altered to deal with children of different ages and capacities. Standardization of the measure is the only way to get around these variations in procedures and most behavioral observations have not been used with enough children to be standardized.

## THE EFFECTS OF THERAPY AND SCHOOL PLACEMENTS

According to parental report, the majority of the developmentally disabled children in this sample were involved in at least some forms of therapy. The only information about therapy collected in this study was from brief, retrospective reports from parents. We decided not to collect more extensive data because there was no way to ensure the accuracy of data recalled over such a long period of time. Moreover, the only conclusive way to determine the effects of therapies is with randomized intervention and control procedures. Because of selection factors in the treatments that children experience, correlational studies require that many associated factors be covaried and, even then, conclusions need to be qualified.

This difficulty is evident in the comparisons of peer engagement across different types of playgrounds. The results suggests that the peer engagement of children with autism is superior on integrated playgrounds. The characteristics of the schools, however, are confounded with the characteristics of the children in this correlational study so that a randomized design is needed.

## LIMITATIONS OF THE STUDY

One of the major limitations of this study is that both the sample and the measures change over time. At any time period, and across time, the samples varied. For example, even at intake, a smaller number of participants was administered the nonverbal communication scales than the play observations, as nonverbal communication was not investigated in our very first study. Each follow-up resulted in the loss of participants, and the same participants were not available for all assessments at the long-term follow-up because families moved out of state. (At one point, we seemed to have a subject in every state beginning with the letter "M," none of which were contiguous.) Some families were only willing for us to see their children at home or in the institutions in which they were living, some children were not cooperative or testable with some measures, and some schools would not allow playground observations. Throughout this monograph, the numbers of participants administered different procedures have been provided. The sample sizes across ages are sufficient, at least for the autistic and Down syndrome groups, and matching has been possible for all group comparisons.

Similarly, measures of even the same constructs change across participants and across time. Part of this is due to historical changes such as those in the standards and methods available for diagnosis of autism or the redesign of developmental assessments. The decision whether to continue to use a somewhat outmoded developmental assessment or to change to a newly standardized measure midstream (when the stream is many years long) has sometimes been determined by formidable outside pressure for currently standardized developmental assessments. Part of the reason for change is due to the fact that few measures cover a broad range of development so that, for example, different language measures must be administered to children of different language abilities. Although behavioral measures can be administered to wider ranges of children, even these must be modified to be used over time. To some extent, then, the findings depend on assumptions that different measures reflect similar constructs.

## CLINICAL AND RESEARCH IMPLICATIONS

Three avenues for intervention can be suggested based on these research findings. First, peer engagement might be increased by encouraging special education teachers to take a more active role in fostering social interaction on the school playground and in informal parts of the classroom program. At present, very few teachers spend any time on the playground, and the aides who are present do not seem to see the encouragement of peer play as part of their responsibilities. Social engagement, however, is crucial for all children and should especially be an area of focus in the educational program of developmentally disabled children. Our observations showed that all the children initiated interaction very infrequently and that the degree of peer engagement depended on these initiations and their reception. The results of this study suggest that adults should help children with autism and Down syndrome to initiate social bids and accept the bids of others.

Second, at least for the children with autism, social skills training that focuses on very basic level social understanding might help to increase social interactions. For children with autism, reading the social and emotional cues of others is clearly very difficult and must make their time in groups extremely challenging. Social comprehension may need to be approached very didactically. There is no doubt that some individuals with autism are able to work around their lack of social understanding by using cognitive mediation.

At present, intervention programs are focused primarily in the early years of life and taper off as children enter the mid-school years. Some of the declines noted in the children over the period of the longitudinal study might be prevented with the maintenance of more intensive interventions. For example, early interventions with children with Down syndrome have been successful in promoting earlier achievements in these children. Gains cannot be maintained, however, if interventions are not continued over time as the complexity of the tasks to be mastered increases with age.

In terms of early intervention, it may be beneficial to target the development of nonverbal communication and representational play early in life. Particularly for children with autism, it is important to find ways to improve these skills as they appear to be prerequisites for later language development and social competence. At this point, environmental correlates of these capacities have not been investigated. We plan to continue this line of investigation, using both correlational and experimental approaches to determine the best means of enhancing the early communicative and play abilities of children with autism and Down syndrome and, ultimately, measure the impact these efforts have on later social competence in these groups.

This research program illustrates the strengths of the developmental approach in investigating the functioning of children with various disabilities. Drawing from the research literature on typical development, we have been able to illuminate the strengths and limitations of social competence in children with autism and Down syndrome (see also Sigman & Capps, 1997). There is a pressing need for more information about the interactions and relationships of developmentally disabled children; we have discussed the kinds of laboratory studies of peer interactions that would be very valuable for understanding and helping the developmentally disabled. Developmental theories and methods are critical to the understanding of what happens to social functioning in children and should be used much more broadly for understanding clinical problems. At the same time, the study of children with developmental disabilities illustrates the consequences of breakdowns in the developmental process when children do not acquire early capacities to communicate and play. Thus, the results of the study of children with autism suggest that early communicative and representational skills may be critical for the acquisition of language. In the absence of these skills, children with autism seem unable to develop much comprehension of language or ability to talk. Both developmental and clinical approaches to the links between these skills are needed to help remedy this serious deficiency.

# REFERENCES

Adamson, L., & Bakeman, R. (1985). Affect and attention: Infants observed with mothers and peers. *Child Development*, **56**, 582–593.

American Psychiatric Association. (1980). *Diagnostic and statistical manual of mental disorders* (3rd ed.). Washington, DC: Author.

American Psychiatric Association. (1987). *Diagnostic and statistical manual of mental disorders* (3rd ed. rev.). Washington, DC: Author.

Bates, E., Benigni, L., Bretherton, I., Camaioni, L., & Volterra, V. (1979). *The emergence of symbols: Cognition and communication in infancy*. New York: Academic Press.

Beckwith, L., & Thompson, S. (1976). Recognition of verbal labels of pictured objects and events by 17- to 30-month-old infants. *Journal of Speech and Hearing Research*, **19**, 690–699.

Berry, P., Gunn, P., & Andrews, R. (1984). The behaviors of Down's syndrome children using the "lock box": A research note. *Journal of Psychology and Psychiatry*, **25**, 125–131.

Brooks-Gunn, J., & Lewis, M. (1982). Development of play behavior in handicapped and normal infants. *Topics in Early Childhood Special Education*, **2**, 14–27.

Bretherton, I. (1991). Intentional communication and the development of an understanding of mind. In D. Frye & C. Moore (Eds.), *Children's theories of mind: Mental states and social understanding* (pp. 271–289). Hillsdale, NJ: Lawrence Erlbaum.

Bruner, J. (1975). From communication to language: A psychological perspective. *Cognition*, **3**, 255–287.

Bruner, J., & Sherwood, V. (1983). Thought, language, and interaction in infancy. In J. Call, E. Galenson, & R. Tyson (Eds.), *Frontiers of infant psychiatry* (pp. 38–55). New York: Basic Books.

Bzoch, K., & League, R. (1971). *Assessing language skills in infancy*. Baltimore: University Park Press.

Cantwell, D. P., Baker, L., Rutter, M., & Mawhood, L. (1989). Infantile autism and developmental receptive dysphasia: A comparative follow up into middle childhood. *Journal of Child Psychology and Psychiatry*, **19**, 19–33.

Carr, J. (1988). Six weeks to twenty-one years old: A longitudinal study of children with Down syndrome and their families. *Journal of Child Psychology and Psychiatry*, **29**, 407–431.

Chung, S. Y., Luk, S. L., & Lee, W. H. (1990). A follow-up study of infantile autism in Hong Kong. *Journal of Autism and Developmental Disorders*, **20**, 221–232.

Corona, R., Dissanayake, C., Arbelle, S., Wellington, P., & Sigman, M. (1998). Is affect aversive to children with autism?: Behavioral and cardiac responses to experimenter distress. *Child Development*, **69**, 1494–1502.

Curcio, F. (1978). Sensorimotor functioning and communication in mute autistic children. *Journal of Autism and Childhood Schizophrenia*, **8**, 282–292.

DeMyer, M. K., Barton, S., DeMyer, W. E., Norton, J. A., Allen, J., & Steele, R. (1973). Prognosis in autism: A follow-up study. *Journal of Autism and Childhood Schizophrenia*, **3**, 199–246.

Dissanayake, C., Sigman, M., & Kasari, C. (1996). Long-term stability of individual differences in the emotional responsiveness of children with autism. *Journal of Child Psychology and Psychiatry*, **37**, 461–467.

Dykens, E. M., Hodapp, R. M., & Evans, D. W. (1994). Profiles and development of adaptive behavior in children with Down syndrome. *American Journal on Mental Retardation*, **98**, 580–587.

Eisenberg, L. (1956). The autistic child in adolescence. *American Journal of Psychiatry*, **112**, 607–612.

Fowler, A. E. (1995). Linguistic variability in persons with Down syndrome: Research and implications. In L. Nadel & D. Rosenthal (Eds.), *Down syndrome: Living and learning in the community* (pp. 121–131). New York: Wiley-Liss.

Fowler, A. E., Gelman, R., & Gleitman, L. R. (1994). The course of language learning in children with Down syndrome. In H. Tager-Flusberg (Ed.), *Constraints on language learning: Studies of atypical children*. Hillsdale, NJ: Erlbaum.

Frith, U. (1989). *Autism: Explaining the enigma*. Oxford, UK: Basil Blackwell Ltd.

Gillberg, C., & Steffenburg, S. (1987). Outcome and prognostic factors in infantile autism and similar conditions: A population-based study of 46 cases followed through puberty. *Journal of Autism and Developmental Disorders*, **17**, 273–288.

Goldfarb, W. (1970). A follow-up investigation of schizophrenic children treated in residence. *Psychosocial Process*, **1**, 9–64.

Goldstein, D. J., Fogle, E. E., Weber, J. L., & O'Shea, T. M. (1995). Comparison of the Bayley Scales of Infant Development-Second Edition and the Bayley Scales of Infant Development with premature infants. *Journal of Psychoeducational Assessment*, **13**, 391–396.

Guralnick, M. J. (1986). The peer relations of young handicapped and nonhandicapped children. In P. S. Strain, M. J. Guralnick, & H. M. Walker (Eds.), *Children's Social Behavior: Development, Assessment, and Modification* (pp. 93–140). New York: Academic Press.

Guralnick, M. J., & Groom, J. M. (1985). Correlates of peer-related social competence of developmentally delayed preschool children. *American Journal of Mental Deficiency*, **90**, 140–150.

Guralnick, M. J., & Groom, J. M. (1987). Dyadic peer interactions of mildly delayed and nonhandicapped preschool children. *American Journal of Mental Deficiency*, **92**, 178–193.

Guralnick, M. J., & Weinhouse, E. M. (1984). Peer-related social interactions of developmentally delayed young children: Development and characteristics. *Developmental Psychology*, **20**, 815–827.

Hauck, M., Fein, D., Waterhouse, L., & Feinstein, C. (1995). Social initiations by autistic children to adults and other children. *Journal of Autism and Developmental Disorders*, **25**, 579–595.

Hindley, C. B., & Owen, C. F. (1978). The extent of individual changes in I. Q. for ages between 6 months and 17 years, in a British longitudinal sample. *Journal of Child Psychology and Psychiatry*, **19**, 329–350.

Howes, C. (1980). Peer play scale as an index of complexity of peer interaction. *Developmental Psychology*, **16**, 371–372.

Howes, C. (1987). Peer interaction of young children. *Monographs of the Society for Research in Child Development*, **53**(1, Serial No. 217).

Howes, C., & Rodning, C. (1990). Attachment security and social pretend play negotiations: Illustrative study #5. In C. Howes (Ed.), *The social construction of pretend: Social pretend play function* (pp. 89–95). Albany, NY: SUNY Press.

Kanner, L. (1971). Follow-up study of 11 autistic children originally reported in 1943. *Journal of Autism and Childhood Schizophrenia*, **1**, 119–145.

Kasari, C., Freeman, S., Mundy, P., & Sigman, M. (1995). Attention regulation by infants with Down syndrome: An examination of coordinated joint attention and social referencing. *American Journal on Mental Retardation*, **100**, 128–136.

Kasari, C., Mundy, P., Yirmiya, N., & Sigman, M. (1990). Affect and attention in children with Down syndrome. *American Journal on Mental Retardation*, **5**, 55–67.

Krakow, J. B., & Kopp, C. B. (1983). The effects of developmental delay on sustained attention in young children. *Child Development*, **54**, 1143–1155.

Krug, D. A., Arick, J. R., & Almond, P. J. (1980). *Autism Screening Instrument for Education Planning*. Portland, Oregon: AISEP Educational Company.

Landry, S. H., & Chapieski, M. L. (1990). Joint attention of six-month-old Down syndrome and preterm infants: I. Attention to toys and to mother. *American Journal on Mental Retardation*, **94**, 488–498.

Le Couteur, A., Rutter, M., Lord, C., Rios, P., Robertson, S., Holdrafer, M., & McLennan, J. (1989). Autism diagnostic interview: A standardized investigator-based instrument. *Journal of Autism and Developmental Disorders*, **19**, 363–387.

Lord, C., & Hopkins, J. M. (1986). The social behavior of autistic children with younger and same-age nonhandicapped peers. *Journal of Autism and Developmental Disorders*, **16**, 249–262.

Lord, C., & Magill-Evans, J. (1995). Peer interactions of autistic children and adolescents. *Development and Psychopathology*, **7**, 611–626.

Lord, C., Rutter, M., & Le Couteur, A. (1994). Autism Diagnostic Instrument-Revised: A revised version of a diagnostic interview for caregivers of individuals with possible pervasive developmental disorders. *Journal of Autism and Developmental Disorders*, **24**, 659–685.

Lord, C., & Schopler, E. (1989a). Stability of assessment results of autistic and non-autistic language-impaired children from preschool years to early school age. *Journal of Child Psychology and Psychiatry*, **30**, 575–590.

Lord, C., & Schopler, E. (1989b). The role of age at assessment, development level, and test in the stability of intelligence scores in young autistic children. *Journal of Autism and Developmental Disorders*, **19**, 483–499.

Lord, C., & Venter, A. (1992). Outcome and follow-up studies of high-functioning autistic individuals. In E. Schopler & G. B. Mesibov (Eds.), *High-functioning individuals with autism. Current issues in autism* (pp. 187–199). New York: Plenum Press.

Lotter, V. (1974). Factors related to outcome in autistic children. *Journal of Autism and Childhood Schizophrenia*, **4**, 263–277.

Lotter, V. (1978). Follow-up studies. In M. Rutter & E. Schopler (Eds.), *Autism: A reappraisal of concepts and treatment* (pp. 475–495). New York: Plenum Press.

Loveland, K. A., & Kelley, M. L. (1988). Development of adaptive behavior in adolescents and young adults with autism and Down syndrome. *American Journal on Mental Retardation*, **93**, 84–92.

Lynch, M. P., Oller, D. K., Steffens, M. L., Levine, S. L., Basinger, D. L., & Umbel, V. (1995). Onset of speech-like vocalizations in infants with Down syndrome. *American Journal on Mental Retardation*, **100**, 68–86.

MacTurk, R., Vietze, P., McCarthy, M., McQuiston, S., & Yarrow, L. (1985). The organization of exploratory behavior in Down syndrome and nondelayed infants. *Child Development*, **58**, 573–581.

Mervis, C. B. (1988). Early lexical development: Theory and application. In L. Nadel (Ed.), *The psychobiology of Down syndrome* (pp. 101–143). Cambridge, MA: MIT Press.

Miller, J. F. (1988). The developmental asynchrony of language development in children with Down syndrome. In L. Nadel (Ed.), *The psychobiology of Down syndrome* (pp. 167–198). Cambridge, MA: MIT Press.

Miller, J. F., & Chapman, R. S. (1984). Disorders of communication: Investigating the development of language of mentally retarded children. *American Journal of Mental Deficiency*, **88**, 536–545.

Mittler, P., Gilles, S., & Jukes, E. (1966). Prognosis in psychotic children: Report of a follow up study. *Journal of Mental Deficiency Research*, **10**, 73–83.

Mundy, P., Hogan, A., & Doehring, P. (1996). A Preliminary Manual for the Abridged Early Social Communication Scale (ESCS). Unpublished manuscript.

Mundy, P., Kasari, C., Sigman, M., & Ruskin, E. (1995). Nonverbal communication and early language acquisition in children with Down syndrome or normal development. *Journal of Speech and Hearing Disorders*, **38**, 157–167.

Mundy, P., Sigman, M., & Kasari, C. (1994). Joint attention, developmental level and symptom presentation in autism. *Development and Psychopathology*, **6**, 389–401.

Mundy, P., Sigman, M., Kasari, C., & Yirmiya, N. (1988). Nonverbal communication skills in Down syndrome children. *Child Development*, **59**, 235–249.

Mundy, P., Sigman, M., Ungerer, J., & Sherman, T. (1986). Defining the social deficits of autism: The contribution of nonverbal communication measures. *Journal of Child Psychology and Psychiatry*, **27**, 657–669.

Piaget, J. (1952). *The origins of intelligence in children*. New York: International Universities Press.

Piper, M. C., Gendron, M., & Mazer, B. (1986). Developmental profile of Down's syndrome infants receiving early intervention. *Child Care, Health and Development*, **12**, 183–194.

Rauh, H., Rudinger, G., Bowman, T. G., Berry, P., Gunn, P. V., & Hayes, A. (1991). The development of Down's syndrome children. In M. D. Lamb & H. Keller (Eds.), *Infant development: Perspectives from German-speaking countries* (pp. 329–355). Hillsdale, NJ: Erlbaum.

Reynell, J. K. (1977). *Reynell Developmental Language Scales*. Windsor, UK: NFER Publishing Co.

Rodrigue, J. R., Morgan, S. B., & Geffken, G. R. (1991). A comparative evaluation of adaptive behavior in children and adolescents with autism, Down syndrome and normal development. *American Journal on Mental Retardation*, **21**, 187–196.

Ruskin, E., Kasari, C., Mundy, P., & Sigman, M. (1994). Attention to people and toys during social and object mastery in children with Down syndrome. *American Journal on Mental Retardation*, **99**, 103–111.

Ruskin, E., Mundy, P., Kasari, C., & Sigman, M. (1994). Object mastery motivation in children with Down syndrome. *American Journal on Mental Retardation*, **98**, 499–509.

Rutter, M. (1970). Autistic children: Infancy to adulthood. *Seminars in Psychiatry*, **2**, 435–450.

Rutter, M. & Lockyer, L. (1967). A five-to-fifteen-year follow-up study of infantile psychosis. I. Description of sample. *British Journal of Psychiatry*, **113**, 1169–1182.

Schopler, E., Reichler, R. J., & Renner, B. R. (1986). *The Childhood Autism Rating Scale*. New York: Irvington Publishers.

Seibert, J. M., Hogan, A. E., & Mundy, P. C. (1982). Assessing interactional competencies: The Early Social-Communication Scales. *Infant Mental Health Journal*, **3**, 244–245.

Semel, E., Wiig, E. H., & Secord, W. (1987). *Clinical Evaluation of Language Fundamentals–Revised*. San Antonio: The Psychological Corporation.

Serafica, F. C. (1990). Peer relations of children with Down syndrome. In D. Ciccheti & M. Beeghly (Eds.), *Children with Down syndrome: A developmental perspective* (pp. 369–398). Cambridge: Cambridge University Press.

Sigman, M. & Capps, L. (1997). *Children with autism: A developmental perspective*. Cambridge, MA: Harvard University Press.

Sigman, M., Mundy, P., Sherman, T., & Ungerer, J. (1986). Social interactions of autistic, mentally retarded and normal children and their caregivers. *Journal of Child Psychology and Psychiatry*, **27**, 647–656.

Sigman, M., & Ungerer, J. (1981). Sensorimotor skills and language comprehension in autistic children. *Journal of Abnormal Child Psychology*, **9**, 149–165.

Sigman, M., & Ungerer, J. (1984). Cognitive and language skills in autistic, mentally retarded, and normal children. *Developmental Psychology*, **20**, 293–302.

Sigman, M. D., Kasari, C., Kwon, J., & Yirmiya, N. (1992). Responses to the negative emotions of others by autistic, mentally retarded, and normal children. *Child Development*, **63**, 796–807.

Sloper, P., & Turner, S. (1996). Progress in social-independent functioning of young people with Down's syndrome. *Journal of Intellectual Disability Research*, **40**, 39–48.

Smith, L., & von Tetzchner, S. (1986). Communicative, sensorimotor, and language skills of young children with Down syndrome. *American Journal of Mental Deficiency*, **91**, 57–66.

Stone, W. L., & Caro-Martinez, L. M. (1990). Naturalistic observations of spontaneous communication in autistic children. *Journal of Autism and Developmental Disorders*, **20**, 437–453.

Strain, P. S. (1984). Social interactions of handicapped preschoolers. In T. Field, J. L. Roopnarine, & M. Segal (Eds.), *Friendships in Normal and Handicapped Children*. Norwood, NJ: Ablex Publishing Corp.

Strain, P. S. (1995). Social and nonsocial determinants of acceptability in handicapped preschool children. *Topics in Early Childhood Special Education*, **4**, 47–58.

Tager-Flusberg, H. (1986). Constraints on the representation of word meaning: Evidence from autistic and mentally retarded children. In S. Kuczaj & M. Barrett (Eds.), *The development of word meaning* (pp. 139–166). New York: Springer-Verlag.

Thorndike, R. (1972). *Stanford-Binet Intelligence Scale*. Boston: Houghton Mifflin.

Thorndike, R. L., Hagen, E. P., & Sattler, J. M. (1986). *The Stanford Binet Intelligence Scale*. Chicago, IL: Riverside Publishing Company.

Tomasello, M. (1997). Joint attention as social cognition. In C. Moore & P. Dunham (Eds.), *Joint attention: Its origins and role in development*. Hillsdale, NJ: Lawrence Erlbaum.

Ungerer, J. A., & Sigman, M. (1981). Symbolic play and language comprehension in autistic children. *Journal of the American Academy of Child Psychiatry*, **20**, 318–338.

Vaughn, B. E., Contreras, J., & Seifer, R. (1994). Short-term longitudinal study of maternal ratings of temperament in samples of children with Down syndrome and children who are developing normally. *American Journal on Mental Retardation*, **98**, 607–618.

Venter, A., Lord, C., & Schopler, E. (1992). A follow-up study of high-functioning autistic children. *Journal of Child Psychology and Psychiatry*, **33**, 489–507.

Volkmar, F. R., Sparrow, S. S., Gourgreau, D., Cicchetti, D. V., Paul, R., & Cohen, D. J. (1987). Social deficits in autism: An operational approach using the Vineland Adaptive Behavior Scales. *Journal of the American Academy of Child and Adolescent Psychiatry*, **26**, 156–161.

Vygotsky, L. (1978). *Mind in society*. Cambridge, MA: Harvard University Press.

Wang, P. B., & Bellugi, U. (1994). Evidence from two genetic syndromes for a dissociation between verbal and visual-spatial short-term memory. *Journal of Clinical and Experimental Neuropsychology*, **16**, 317–322.

Weisz, J. R., & Zigler, E. (1979). Cognitive development in retarded and non-retarded persons: Piagetian tests of similar structure hypotheses. *Psychological Bulletin*, **86**, 831–851.

Werner, H., & Kaplan, B. (1963). *Symbol formation*. New York: Wiley.

Wiig, E. H., Secord, W., & Semel, E. (1992). *Clinical Evaluation of Language Fundamental-Preschool*. San Antonio: The Psychological Corporation.

Wishart, J. G., & Duffy, L. (1990). Instability of performance on cognitive tests in infants and young children with Down's syndrome. *British Journal of Educational Psychology*, **60**, 10–22.

# ACKNOWLEDGMENTS

The research summarized in this monograph has been supported by Grant NS25243 from the National Institute of Neurological Diseases and Stroke and by Grant HD17662 and Program Project Grant HD-DCD35470 from the National Institute of Child Health and Human Development and the National Institute of Deafness and Communication Disorders. Five individuals made enormous sequential contributions to this research program: Judy Ungerer, Ph.D., who studied early play and cognitive development; Peter Mundy, Ph.D., who focused on nonverbal communication; Connie Kasari, Ph.D., who investigated social interactions; Nurit Yirmiya, Ph.D., who researched affective responses; and Lisa Capps, Ph.D., who concentrated on social understanding. We are grateful for the assistance of Dr. Betty Jo Freeman in helping us to recruit participants. Many talented research assistants have worked on this research program over the years. The most recent include Cristina Fernandez, Jennifer Kehres, Donna Liu, Nicholas Lofthous, and Michael Siller. As always, we are indebted to Margie Greenwald for her organizational and administrative assistance. Finally, we thank the families who have shared their children, their observations, and their insights with us.

Correspondence should be addressed to Marian Sigman, Ph.D., 68237, Department of Psychiatry, UCLA School of Medicine, Los Angeles, California 90024.

# COMMENTARY

METHODOLOGICAL ISSUES IN CROSS-SYNDROME COMPARISONS:
MATCHING PROCEDURES, SENSITIVITY (*Se*), AND SPECIFICITY (*Sp*)

*Carolyn B. Mervis and Byron F. Robinson*

The research described in Sigman and Ruskin's monograph represents
an enormous undertaking. The numbers of children included in the initial
autism and Down syndrome groups are among the largest ever reported for
a single study involving special populations, and the sample sizes in the long
term follow-up (after an average of 8 or 9 years) make this project perhaps
the largest longitudinal investigation of children with autism or Down syndrome. Thus, this opportunity to study continuity and change in language
and other aspects of social competence for children with these syndromes is
unprecedented.

The most exciting findings are the within-participant results for the
children with autism, with regard to joint attention. The theoretical importance of the ability to engage in joint attention episodes for the onset and development of language has been stressed repeatedly: By providing the basis
for a shared referential framework, episodes of joint attention help the child
to determine the reference of the adult's utterance, and thereby begin to acquire language (see, e.g., Carpenter, Nagell, & Tomasello, 1998). Both concurrent relations and short-term (up to 10 months) longitudinal relations
between amount of joint attention and language acquisition have been demonstrated for toddlers who are developing normally (e.g., Carpenter et al.,
1998; Smith, Adamson, & Bakeman 1988; Tomasello & Todd, 1983). In

Preparation of this manuscript was supported by grant HD29957 from the National
Institute of Child Health and Human Development and by grant NS35102 from the National Institute of Neurological Disorders and Stroke. Please address correspondence to
Carolyn Mervis, Department of Psychology, University of Louisville, Louisville, KY 40292
or cbmervis@louisville.edu.

addition, as described in Chapter III, Sigman and her colleagues have previously demonstrated a concurrent relation between joint attention and language ability for a relatively small sample of young children with autism.

Because of the longitudinal nature of the current study, Sigman and Ruskin have been able to measure not only concurrent relations (at an average age of 3 years 11 months) between joint attention and language, but also to consider the relation between early levels of joint attention and language ability 1 year later and (on average) 9 years later (mean age 12 years 10 months). As expected, Sigman and Ruskin found significant concurrent relations between language age and both frequency of initiating joint attention and frequency of responding to the researcher's bids (pointing, combined with calling the child's name) for joint attention. The measures of joint attention obtained at the initial time point also were significantly correlated with language age 1 year later, even after partialling out initial expressive language age and chronological age (CA). Also, after initial language age and CA were partialled out, frequency of responding to joint attention bids at the initial visit still accounted for a significant and substantial portion of the variance (21%) in expressive language age 9 years later.

Sigman and Ruskin also found that for children with autism, early responding to joint attention is related to IQ 9 years later. Most of the children (39) with autism had DQs < 70 at the initial visit. At the final visit, however, 11 of the 39 children had IQs ≥ 70. This group of children had responded to bids for joint attention at the initial visit significantly more often than the children whose IQs remained < 70, even after controlling for initial DQ. The relation between early responding to joint attention and later IQ is likely due in part to the impact of early responding to joint attention on later expressive language. Sigman and Ruskin did not consider whether early joint attention levels were related to either concurrent or later social/emotional responsiveness for the children with autism. (It would be very interesting to know if there are such relations.) They did address the relation between early joint attention and engagement in social play 9 years later; results indicated that for children with autism, both frequency of initiating joint attention and frequency of responding to joint attention were significantly correlated with amount of social play 9 years later. The correlation for initiating joint attention remained significant even after initial DQ was partialled out. Once again, this finding is likely due in part to the relation between joint attention and expressive language acquisition. Therefore, the findings serve to remind us that the impact of expressive language extends well beyond intellectual abilities, to relations with peers. The finding that early joint attention is related not only to concurrent language functioning, but also to both language functioning and social interaction with peers 9 years later, provides the strongest support so far for the theoretical importance of joint attention for the acquisition and practical use of language.

Sigman and Ruskin's project also involved a large number of between-group comparisons; the primary purpose of these was to identify possible deficits in nonverbal communication, symbolic play, language, social/emotional responsiveness, or peer relations, and to determine if these were "specific, universal, and unique" (7) to a particular syndrome. Sigman and Ruskin consider a deficit *specific* to a syndrome if that ability is more impaired than would be expected based on level of other abilities, as determined by a comparison to children with other types of disabilities matched on a control variable (for this project, language age). Thus, if syndrome group A and contrast group B are matched on language age, but group A's mean on a target variable is significantly lower than group B's, then group A is considered to exhibit a *specific* deficit on the target variable. A deficit (or pattern of deficits) is considered *unique* to syndrome A if it is evidenced only by individuals who have syndrome A. If the previously outlined logic for determining specificity is followed for three or more groups (including a contrast group composed of children with mixed or unknown etiologies), and the mean for syndrome group A is significantly lower than the mean for any of the other groups, Sigman and Ruskin consider the deficit *unique* to syndrome A. A deficit is considered *universal* for syndrome A if it is shared by all children with that syndrome (or if there is an explanation for how children who do not have this deficit have compensated for it). Although claims about universality are made, no method is proposed for testing for this characteristic.

We have serious concerns regarding whether the determination of specificity, universality, and uniqueness—which ultimately involve the performance of individuals, rather than groups as a whole—is appropriately addressed by standard between-syndrome comparisons. In the remainder of this commentary, we describe some of the problems with group matching, offer a method of partially correcting them, and then argue that group designs are inherently limited in their effectiveness for identifying characteristics of individuals with a syndrome. Finally, we briefly outline an alternative method for determining specific, unique, and universal characteristics associated with a syndrome. This method is based on consideration of the pattern of performance of individuals, and determining the extent to which such patterns are replicated across individuals with the same syndrome or individuals with different syndromes or etiologies.

## DIFFICULTIES WITH THE GROUP-MATCHING DESIGN

The cross-syndrome comparisons reported in this monograph are based on a group matching design, a type of design that is commonly used in studies of children with disabilities. In this design, two or more groups are matched on a control variable (in this monograph, generally language age), and the groups are compared on one or more target variables. If there are significant differences between groups on the target variable, then Sigman and Ruskin consider any group(s) whose mean value on the target variable is significantly lower than the mean value for other groups to evidence a deficit on the target variable. (The same logic, applied to groups whose mean values were significantly higher than other groups, also could be used to identify strengths.) However, although often used, group matching designs are based on assumptions that are extremely difficult to meet. In this section, we consider two types of problems with group matching designs that are particularly pertinent to developmental studies, especially those involving special populations.

### Problems With Interpreting Findings Due to Matching Procedures

The matching logic requires that participant groups do not differ on the control variable. To ensure this, researchers commonly perform a means difference test, and assume that the groups are matched if they do not differ significantly. This procedure requires the acceptance of the null hypothesis. As Cohen (1990) points out, however, the null hypothesis is almost never literally true. Therefore, we must consider how close is close enough. Usually, researchers set $\alpha$ to the traditional .05 level. Harcum (1990, p. 404) describes this as "casual acceptance of the null hypothesis."[1] Occasionally, as in this monograph, a more conservative $\alpha$ of .10 is used. In terms of the matching design it is not so much the $\alpha$ level, but rather the probability of making a Type II error (accepting the hypothesis that the groups do not differ even though they do) that is of primary concern. For practical purposes, it can be very difficult to estimate accurately the probability of making a Type II error. However, it is known that the larger the $\alpha$ level, the less likely the researcher is to make a Type II error. The question then becomes, how high should $\alpha$ be in order for the researcher to accept the null hypothesis that the groups do not differ on the matching variable? Frick (1995) proposes the following guidelines: Any $p$ value less than .20 is too low to accept the null hypothesis. A $p$ value greater than .50 is large enough to accept the null hypothesis. Finally, $p$ values between .20 and .50 are ambiguous. In the monograph, of

---

[1] Harcum argues that "casual acceptance" of the null hypothesis is unintentionally encouraged by many research methodology textbooks. Because these texts do not discuss the possibility of predicting a null result, they "tacitly encourage" (p. 404) the use of the reverse of the hypothesis testing process. Thus, just as researchers reject the null hypothesis when $p$ is less than $\alpha$ (generally, .05), they are likely to erroneously accept the null hypothesis whenever $p$ is greater than $\alpha$.

seven group matches for language age, the median $p$ value was .14, with a minimum value of .104. Five of the $p$ values were < .20; the remaining two were .20 and .34. Thus, it is likely that for most of the comparisons reported in the monograph, the groups in fact were *not* matched for language age. This is especially a problem for the analyses of joint attention and play (Chapter III) because the autism group both had the youngest mean language age and the lowest value on many of the target variables. Thus, differences between groups may well be due to language age, rather than autism per se.

The problem with failing to adequately match the groups on language age is exacerbated in the comparisons in Chapter III due to the language age range of the children. The language age period between 16 and 20 months is a time of highly nonlinear language growth (e.g., Robinson & Mervis, 1998), both for children who are developing normally and children who have developmental disabilities. Children with a language age of 16 months (the mean language age for the autism group) would be expected to have very small vocabularies, and to be speaking in single words. Children with a language age of 18 months (the mean language age for the Down syndrome group) would be beginning their vocabulary spurt, and starting to produce multiword utterances. Children with a language age of 20 months (the mean language age for the developmentally delayed and typically developing groups) would be expected to be in the midst of their vocabulary spurt and to be producing a large proportion of multiword utterances (Fenson et al., 1994). Note that we are not arguing that children with autism do not have problems with joint attention; we expect that relative to mental age (MA), which would be greater than language age for most children with autism, most children with autism will evidence problems with joint attention. We are not convinced by the results of the present study, however, that the joint attention abilities of children with autism are worse than would be expected for language age, for two reasons. First, it is unlikely that the groups are actually matched for language age. Second, this likely mismatch is further compounded by the fact that the language age range covered by the four groups spans a highly nonlinear period of language growth.

As Sigman and Ruskin point out in Chapter II, CA can confound group-matching designs if the comparison groups differ widely on associated variables due to school settings. The follow-up sample was therefore restricted only to individuals whom the authors expected to be in similar types of school settings (age range 6 to 19 years). There is another way, however, in which CA differences can lead to invalid findings. If the control variable and the target variable develop at different rates, then the differences between the raw scores (and therefore age equivalents) will not be stable across CA. If this is the case, one could not predict that two individuals with identical age equivalents on the control variable but different CAs should have similar scores on the target variable.

The situation in which two or more variables are developing at different rates is not unusual. To illustrate this problem, we have examined the relations between age equivalents on different subtests from the Differential Ability Scales (DAS; Elliott, 1990), as a function of CA. We considered the 6- to 17-year age range, which is slightly less than the 6- to 19-year age range included by Sigman and Ruskin in the follow-up study. We selected an age equivalent of 8 years 3 months (8;3) on the Similarities subtest (corresponding to an ability score of 83) and then compared this to the expected age equivalents for the Definitions, Matrices, Pattern Construction, and Recall of Digits subtests, for different CAs, based on the test norms. Thus, we treated Similarities age equivalent as the control variable, and the age equivalents for the other subtests as target variables. That is, we asked the question, if a child has an age equivalent of 8;3 on the Similarities subtest, and all of his or her abilities are at the same level (i.e., the child earns the same standard score on each subtest), what are his or her predicted age equivalents for each of these other subtests? The resulting graph is presented in Figure 1. As one would expect, if a child's CA is 8;3, and his or her age equivalent on Similarities is

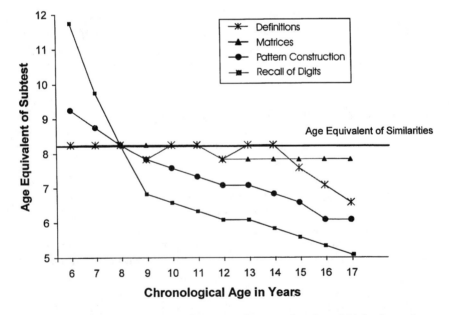

FIGURE 1.—Variability in expected age equivalents as a function of CA for four subtests of the Differential Ability Scales, given a constant age equivalent of 8;3 on the Similarities subtest and the assumption that the child has earned the same standard score on each of the five subtests.

also 8;3, then age equivalents for each of the other subtests would be 8;3 as well. (This child is performing at the median level for his or her CA on Similarities, and would therefore be expected to perform at the median level on each of the other subtests, assuming he or she has equivalent abilities in each of the domains tested.) But what happens when a child's performance on Similarities is either above or below the median for his or her CA? As illustrated in Figure 1, this relation varies as a function of which subtest is the target variable. The relation between Similarities and Matrices age equivalents remains reasonably stable across the entire CA range from 6 to 17 years. Therefore, if Similarities age equivalent was the matching variable and Matrices age equivalent was the target variable, the researcher could sample from a large CA range without invalidating group comparisons. On the other hand, matching on Similarities with Recall of Digits as the target variable would be quite problematic if participants varied in CA. In this case, there is actually a crossover in the relation from 6 to 17 years CA. At 6 years, the expected age equivalent on Recall of Digits is 11;9, much higher than the age equivalent of 8;3 on the control variable. As would be expected, at a CA of 8 years the age equivalent of both subtests is the same. At 17 years of age, however, the expected age equivalent on Recall of Digits predicted by a Similarities age equivalent of 8;3 is much lower: 5;1. Given this pattern of relations, even if groups were matched perfectly on Similarities, one would predict group differences on Recall of Digits, provided there was also a CA difference between the groups.

In the example derived from the Differential Ability Scales, we can identify differential rates of growth between measures because each of the Differential Ability Scales subtests was individually normed on the same group of children. For most laboratory measures, however, such norms are not available. Thus, for example, the expected rates of growth for variables such as joint attention or response to another person's distress relative to the growth curve for language age are unknown. It is therefore difficult to evaluate if any differences across groups in CA confound any of the group comparisons. (That is, the impact of CA could be minimal, as in the Differential Ability Scales example of Similarities age equivalent as the control variable and Matrices age equivalent as the target variable; or could be substantial, as occurs with the same control variable but with Recall of Digits as the target variable.) The possibility that some of the cross-group comparisons in the monograph are uninterpretable due to CA confounds is real, however, because the groups differed significantly in CA. In particular, the autism group was significantly older than either the Down syndrome group or the typically developing group at the initial session. At follow-up 9 years later, the group with autism was significantly older than both the Down syndrome and the developmental delay groups. Furthermore, each syndrome group spanned a wide age range.

121

It is possible to reduce the problem of CA confounds by restricting the age range of the samples to a point where there are no significant differences in the rate of development for the target and control variables. If restricting the CA range is not a desirable option given the research question, pair-wise matching on both the target variable and CA may alleviate the confound. Pair-wise matching involves selecting one individual from the first syndrome group and then finding an individual in the comparison group who both is the same CA and has a similar score on the control variable. If the match is close enough, then the researcher may be confident that differential rates of development in the target and control variables will not confound group differences tests on the target variable. Note that it is not enough to group match on both CA and the control variable; one must ensure that *individuals* are matched on both variables simultaneously.

Pair-wise matching, however, is not appropriate if differences in the relation between the target and control variable exist as a function of syndrome group. Furthermore, because it is necessary to match each pair of children on both CA and the control variable, the problem of generalizability is likely to be exacerbated. As pairs of children who match on *both* CA and the control variable will be more difficult to find than pairs that match on *either* CA *or* the control variable, it is likely that a higher proportion of children in the ascertainment sample will need to be excluded from the final sample due to lack of an appropriate match in the comparison group. Finally, the issue of how closely individuals must be matched on the control variable(s) must still be considered when pair-wise matching.

Although we have raised a number of concerns regarding the group-matching design used in the monograph, we do not mean to imply that all of the cross-syndrome findings are inconclusive. For instance, Sigman and Ruskin report that children with Down syndrome do not exhibit a unique deficit in requesting behaviors. This finding is consistent with our observations of both children who have Down syndrome and children with other developmental disabilities. On the other hand, we cannot evaluate the appropriateness of any of the cross-group comparisons contained in the monograph because we do not have enough information concerning the distributions of control variable scores and CA for the samples used for each statistical test (as well as descriptive statistics for those participants who were dropped). The monograph also does not adequately address the possibility of CA confounds.

### Conceptual Difficulty With Matching Designs

Even if we can be sure that all assumptions are met to produce valid tests of syndrome differences, there is a deeper conceptual concern that the group design does not fully answer questions concerning specificity, uniqueness, and universality. Specificity implies a quality of the individual, not the group. Therefore, when Sigman and Ruskin refer to a specific deficit of joint attention in children with autism, we interpret this to mean that most individuals with autism will have poor joint attention skills relative to their other abilities. When researchers try to identify the most important characteristics of a disorder such as autism, they are basically asking, "What characteristics would disappear if we removed the autism from this child?" Therefore, the perfect control for any child with a syndrome is that same child, but without the syndrome. The closest we can come to this design would perhaps be monozygotic twins reared in the same environment, who are discordant for the syndrome. Such pairs of monozygotic twins do exist. Findings from monozygotic pairs of twins discordant for autism are furthering our understanding of the autistic spectrum, including its language component (e.g., Bailey et al., 1995; Kates et al., 1998; Le Couteur et al., 1996). A few pairs of monozygotic twins discordant for Down syndrome also have been reported (e.g., Rogers, Voullaire, & Gold, 1982). However, the rarity of discordant monozygotic twins for both autism and Down syndrome precludes the possibility of employing the twin method as a realistic design for most research questions concerning these syndromes. Therefore, it is necessary to use some other form of control. In many research designs, and in this monograph, the group-matching method is used to control the effect of potentially confounding variables.

The problem with group difference tests is that they do not precisely answer the specificity question. When we ask questions about specificity of deficits, we want to know first if individuals' ability for the measure in question is lower than their ability for other measures, and then we want to know if most of the individuals within a syndrome group display this tendency. Of course, if the mean of one group is significantly lower on the target variable than the mean of another matched group, then it is likely that some number of individuals in the first group display a particular deficit on the target variable. However, without precise information about the distributions of scores on the target variable for the two groups, we cannot be sure what proportion of individuals shows this deficit. For instance, Sigman and Ruskin found that, as a group, the individuals with autism responded to joint attention at a significantly lower rate than any of the other groups. Examination of Figure 2 in the monograph, however, reveals that the mean level of responding for the typically developing children falls within 1 standard deviation of the autism group. Therefore, if the distributions of scores for level of responding are not skewed, then more than 20% of the children with autism responded to joint attention initiations more frequently than the average typically developing child. If a substantial proportion of individuals with autism respond to joint attention at relatively high levels, one must wonder if response to joint attention is appropriately considered a deficit of autism in general, or if there are subtypes of autism that do not involve such problems. It may even be the case that only a small proportion of children with autism respond so infrequently to joint attention initiation that they would be categorized below low-normal levels. At the very least, the overlap in distributions suggests that joint attention deficits are not universal for children with autism.

Sigman and Ruskin also state that children with Down syndrome have universal deficits in language. However, the authors did not propose a method for determining if a deficit was universal, and never report specific evidence that all children with Down syndrome have language deficits. Although the majority of individuals with Down syndrome do appear to have a specific deficit at least in expressive language (e.g., Chapman, 1997), there also is ample evidence in the literature of children with Down syndrome who have excellent expressive language (e.g., Rondal, 1995; Vallar & Papagno, 1993). A consistent finding emerging from these studies is that individuals with Down syndrome who have good language abilities also have good auditory memory ability. For example, the young woman studied by Rondal had a backward digit span of 4, which is well within the normal range for adults without disabilities. Vallar and Papagno considered both digit span and phonological memory (memory for nonsense syllables), and found that the participant with Down syndrome who had excellent language had both digit span and phonological memory ability within the normal range. In contrast, the other participants with Down syndrome, who had limited language abilities, also had short digit spans and very poor phonological memory. It is important to determine why some individuals with Down syndrome have good language abilities. In fact, one could argue that studying those individuals with Down syndrome who have extraordinary characteristics provides more information concerning the mechanisms underlying development than studying only those individuals with more typical Down syndrome profiles. Clearly then, portraying the universality of a characteristic as all or nothing, and thereby ignoring individual differences within a syndrome, may stymie further research into understanding the typology and mechanisms underlying a developmental disorder.

## ALTERNATE METHOD FOR DETERMINING SPECIFIC, UNIQUE, AND UNIVERSAL CHARACTERISTICS

In the remainder of this paper, we describe a method of identifying characteristics of a syndrome that alleviates many of the concerns we have with the group-matching procedure when used to answer questions about specificity, uniqueness, and universality. The alternate method also provides a methodological parallel to the idea that a specific characteristic is a quality of an individual, not a group of individuals. In this alternate method, we propose that specificity of a characteristic is measured independent of and with different methods from uniqueness and universality. Rather than a group approach, we suggest that specific deficits be defined as abilities that are below the level expected given an individual's other skill levels, regardless of the syndrome group to which he or she belongs. This is achieved by profiling a number of skills for all participants, and then, instead of comparing group means, examining the profile of each individual. For instance, you could measure language variables (e.g., receptive vocabulary, expressive vocabulary), nonverbal skills (e.g., performance on matrices, drawing ability), and joint attention. If joint attention skills are worse than would be predicted by the other abilities, then joint attention is a likely candidate for a specific deficit for that particular individual.

Of course it is necessary to have some common metric by which the individual skills can be compared, for example, subtests taken from a single standardized assessment. Recently, we have proposed a cognitive profile for individuals with Williams syndrome (Frangiskakis et al., 1996; Mervis, Morris, Bertrand, & Robinson, 1999), characterized by a relative strength in auditory rote memory and both relative and absolute weakness in visuospatial construction. Operationalization of this profile is based on the Differential Ability Scales, which provide separate standard scores for each of the subtests. Moreover, the subtest standard scores are based on the same norming sample, thereby allowing us to validly compare a single individual's subtest scores. (For the skill comparisons in a profile to be valid, it is necessary that all assessment measures used be normed on the same sample.) Profiling becomes more difficult for measures that do not already have appropriate norms. The researcher would, in essence, have to create norms for each of the specific target variables. These norms could be restricted, however, to the CA and ability levels of interest for the research question(s) being addressed, and could be gathered either before or after completing the special populations component of the research.

The advantage of the profiling method is that aspects of a profile are identified relative to the other skills of the individual rather than in comparison to another syndrome group. This approach decreases the likelihood that a characteristic will appear unique simply because the opposite characteristic is evidenced by the contrast syndrome. For instance, Bellugi and her colleagues (e.g., Bellugi, Marks, Bihrle, & Sabo, 1988; Bellugi, Wang, & Jernigan, 1994) have argued that individuals with Williams syndrome, despite having significant mental retardation, have extraordinary or intact language abilities. This claim is based on comparisons of people with Williams syndrome to one contrast group, Down syndrome. The actual case, however, is that, rather than people with Williams syndrome having *better* language abilities than would be expected, individuals with Down syndrome have *weaker* expressive language abilities than would be expected for overall level of cognitive abilities (e.g., Morris & Mervis, 1999). When compared to groups of children with mental retardation (of mixed or unknown etiology) matched for IQ and CA, the language abilities of the Williams syndrome group are generally consistent with those of the contrast group (e.g., Gosch, Stading, & Pankau, 1994; Udwin & Yule, 1990). Our within-participant comparisons of children with Williams syndrome indicate that for the majority, expressive vocabulary ability is not significantly better than expected based on overall cognitive abilities. In particular, we considered the performance of 39 4- to 7-year-olds with Williams syndrome on the Preschool Differential Ability Scales. For 29 (74%), standard score on the naming vocabulary subtest was consistent with overall standard score (GCA; similar to IQ; Mervis & Robinson, unpublished data).

Another advantage of the profiling method is that it allows the researcher to control for a large number of variables without the difficulties of matching. As long as a common metric (i.e., norms developed with a single sample of individuals) exists for all of the variables for which the researcher wishes to control, there is no need to attempt multivariate matching with other syndrome groups. Thus, the researcher is not exposed to the aforementioned problems with generalizability.

Once individual profiles and specific characteristics have been identified, systematic examination of uniqueness and universality is feasible. Borrowing from signal-detection and epidemiological methods (Siegel, Vukicevic, Elliott, & Kraemer, 1989), we prefer the terms sensitivity ($Se$) and specificity ($Sp$) to refer to universality and uniqueness. To discriminate between Sigman and Ruskin's use of the term "specificity" and the traditional definition, we will refer to specificity as defined below using the symbol $Sp$ and continue to spell out the word when referring to Sigman and Ruskin's definition. Given samples of two groups, those with the syndrome of interest (target group) and those without the syndrome (contrast group), $Se$ is defined as the proportion of individuals in the target group who display the characteristic. For instance, in a sample of 50 children with autism, if 39 displayed deficits of joint attention, then the $Se$ of joint attention as a characteristic of autism would be .78. On the other hand, $Sp$ is defined as the proportion of individuals without the syndrome who *do not* possess the characteristic. Therefore, if 132 individuals in a group of 150 children with heterogeneous developmental delays, Down syndrome, or normal development did not display a deficit of joint attention, then the characteristic would possess a $Sp$ of 0.88.

Rather than simply stating that a characteristic is or is not unique or universal, reporting levels of $Se$ and $Sp$ gives readers a sense of how well the characteristic represents individuals with a particular syndrome. For instance, Sigman and Ruskin state that deficits in joint attention are unique and universal in children with autism (104). This implies that *all* children with autism display the deficit and that no individual from another syndrome group would be expected to have problems with joint attention. Because *Se* and *Sp* range from 0 to 1.00, they provide a metric by which to measure just how unique and universal a characteristic is. Thus, it is likely the case that both *Se* and *Sp* are high for children with autism relative to other syndrome groups, but that they are not 1.00. For instance, if the *Se* for deficits in joint attention is .85, we would know that this is an important characteristic of autism, but that not all individuals with autism will have such deficits. Obviously, this is vital information for both researchers interested in identifying the etiology and typologies of autism, and for clinicians attempting to design intervention programs. Additionally, *Se* and *Sp* allow one to compare the efficiency of different characteristics of a syndrome for diagnostic and/or research purposes. For instance, the *Se* of mental retardation for autism is moderately high, but the *Sp* would be very low relative to other neurodevelopmental disorders. Therefore, mental retardation is clearly a characteristic of many (perhaps most) individuals with autism, but is not as central to the syndrome as deficits in joint attention.

*Se* and *Sp* are independent of what Sigman and Ruskin define as specific deficits, and can be applied to any measurable characteristic. Therefore, it is possible to calculate the *Se* and *Sp* of any characteristic, regardless of its specificity. For instance, the *Se* and *Sp* for mental retardation (MR) could be measured for individuals with Down syndrome relative to a contrast group of individuals with other neurodevelopmental disorders. The likely result is that MR would have a high *Se* (i.e., most individuals with Down syndrome would have MR), but very low *Sp* (many of the individuals in the neurodevelopmental disorders contrast group also would have MR). A characteristic profile (which may include both strengths and weaknesses) for a syndrome would be one that most individuals with the syndrome fit, and most other individuals do not. In other words, one goal of a profile is to maximize *Se* and *Sp*. Although there is not sufficient space in this commentary to describe the procedure, Receiver Operator Curve (ROC) analysis is a tool that can be used to find characteristics that maximize *Se* and *Sp* values (Kraemer, 1988). The method can be modified to take into account more than one characteristic at a time (see Mervis et al., 1999).

The two-step method we have described alleviates many of the problems with the group-matching design. First, because there is no matching procedure, there are no problems with generalizability as long as the ascertainment strategy was valid. Furthermore, the method we propose allows the researcher to consider as many variables as he or she desires to include in the profile. Because the individual acts as his or her own control, there also are no difficulties in interpreting findings due to lack of match between groups. CA confounds are not a problem if CA-based standard scores are used in the profiling. Finally, the alternate method proposed here is conceptually more satisfying in that it defines specific deficits (or strengths, or patterns of strengths and weaknesses) at the level of the individual and only then contrasts syndromes at the group level to determine $Se$ and $Sp$. It is important to remember, however, that $Sp$ levels can differ dramatically, depending on the makeup of the contrast group. For instance, if the target group was Down syndrome and the contrast group was males with Fragile X syndrome, the $Sp$ for MR would be very low. If the contrast group was typically developing children, however, $Sp$ would be very high. Therefore $Sp$ and uniqueness can only be appropriately determined if a large contrast group (or groups) is used, which includes adequate representation of those syndromes that are most likely to be similar to the target syndrome on the variables of interest.

## SUMMARY

We are impressed with the magnitude and potential importance of the studies presented by Sigman and Ruskin in this monograph. The within-syndrome findings for the children with autism concerning relations between early joint attention and a range of cognitive abilities a full 9 years later provide the strongest evidence so far that early nonverbal communication skills play an important role in the later development of language, intelligence, and social relations with peers. The purpose of the monograph was not limited to within-syndrome research questions, however. Sigman and Ruskin state that a major goal of the research reported in the monograph was to identify specific, unique, and universal deficits for autism and Down syndrome. They base their method of identifying such syndrome characteristics on the group-matching procedure. Given that this procedure is fraught with difficulties, we are concerned that many of Sigman and Ruskin's cross-syndrome comparisons may be incorrect. We do not mean to single out Sigman and Ruskin. The group-matching method is frequently used in special populations research, with the null hypothesis of no differences on the control variable being accepted at dangerously low $p$ values. Our concerns with the group-matching problem extend to much of the extant research that attempts to identify characteristics of individuals based on the performance of their syndrome group relative to a control group. The profiling procedure we outlined seems more fruitful and conceptually satisfying than the traditional matching method. When profiling is not possible, however, it is important to consider the impact of CA confounds and statistical decision procedures used to ensure matching on the control variable, when interpreting syndrome differences on variables of interest.

## REFERENCES

Bailey, A., Le Couteur, A., Gottesman, I., Bolton, P., Simonoff, E., Yuzda, E., & Rutter, M. (1995). Autism as a strongly genetic disorder: Evidence from a British twin study. *Psychology and Medicine*, **25**, 63–77.

Bellugi, U., Marks, S., Bihrle, A., & Sabo, H. (1988). Dissociation between language and cognitive functions in Williams syndrome. In D. Bishop & K. Mogford (Eds.), *Language development in exceptional circumstances* (pp. 177–189). Edinburgh: Churchill Livingstone.

Bellugi, U., Wang, P. P., & Jernigan, T. L. (1994). Williams syndrome: An unusual neuropsychological profile. In S. H. Broman & J. Grafman (Eds.), *Atypical cognitive deficits in developmental disorders: Implications for brain function* (pp. 23–56). Hillsdale, NJ: Erlbaum.

Carpenter, M., Nagell, K., & Tomasello, M. (1998). Social cognition, joint attention, and communicative competence from 9 to 15 months of age. *Monographs of the Society for Research in Child Development*, **63**(No. 4, Serial no. 255).

Chapman, R. S. (1997). Language development in children and adolescents with Down syndrome. *Mental Retardation and Developmental Disabilities Research Reviews*, **3**, 307–312.

Cohen, J. (1990). Things I have learned (so far). *American Psychologist*, **45**, 1304–1312.

Elliott, C. D. (1990) *Differential Ability Scales*. San Diego: Harcourt Brace Jovanovich.

Fenson, L., Dale, P. S., Reznick, J. S., Bates, E., Thal, D. J., & Pethick, S. J. (1994). Variability in early communicative development. *Monographs of the Society for Research in Child Development*, **59**(No. 5, Serial no. 242).

Frangiskakis, J. M., Ewart, A. K., Morris, C. A., Mervis, C. B., Bertrand, J., Robinson, B. F., Klein, B. P., Ensing, G. J., Everett, L. A., Green, E. D., Proschel, C., Gutowski, N., Noble, M., Atkinson, D. L., Odelberg, S. J., & Keating, M. T. (1996). LIM-Kinase1 hemizygosity implicated in impaired visuospatial constructive cognition. *Cell*, **86**, 59–69.

Frick, R. W. (1995). Accepting the null hypothesis. *Memory & Cognition*, **23**, 132–138.

Gosch, A., Stading, G., & Pankau, R. (1994). Linguistic abilities in children with Williams-Beuren syndrome. *American Journal of Medical Genetics*, **52**, 291–296.

Harcum, E. R. (1990). Methodological vs. empirical literature: Two views on the acceptance of the null hypothesis. *American Psychologist*, **45**, 404–405.

Kates, W. R., Mostofsky, S. H., Zimmerman, A. W., Mazzocco, M. M., Landa R., Warsofsky, I. S., Kaufmann, W. E., & Reiss, A. L. (1998). Neuroanatomical and neurocognitive differences in a pair of monozygous twins discordant for strictly defined autism. *Annals of Neurology*, **43**, 782–791.

Kraemer, H. C. (1988). Assessment of 2 × 2 associations: Generalization of signal-detection methodology. *The American Statistician*, **42**, 37–49.

Le Couteur, A., Bailey, A., Goode, S., Pickles, A., Robertson, S., Gottesman, I., & Rutter, M. (1996). A broader phenotype of autism: The clinical spectrum in twins. *Journal of Child Psychology and Psychiatry*, **37**, 785–801.

Mervis, C. B., Morris, C. A., Bertrand, J., & Robinson, B. F. (1999). Williams syndrome: Findings from an integrated program of research. In H. Tager-Flusberg (Ed.), *Neurodevelopmental disorders* (pp. 65–110). Cambridge, MA: MIT Press.

Morris, C. A., & Mervis, C. B. (1999). Williams syndrome. In S. Goldstein & C. Reynolds (Eds.), *Neurodevelopmental and genetic disorders in children* (pp. 555–590). New York: Guilford.

Robinson, B. F., & Mervis, C. B. (1998). Disentangling early language development: Modeling lexical and grammatical acquisition using an extension of case-study methodology. *Developmental Psychology*, **34**, 363–375.

Rogers, J. G., Voullaire, L., & Gold, H. (1982). Monozygotic twins discordant for trisomy 21. *American Journal of Medical Genetics*, **11**, 143–146.

Rondal, J. (1995). *Exceptional language development in Down syndrome*. Cambridge: Cambridge University Press.

Siegel, B., Vukicevic, J., Elliott, G. R., & Kraemer, H. C. (1989). The use of signal detection theory to assess DSM-IIIR criteria for autistic disorder. *Journal of the American Academy of Child & Adolescent Psychiatry*, **28**, 542–548.

Smith, C. B., Adamson, L. B., & Bakeman, R. (1988). Interactional predictors of early language. *First Language*, **8**, 143–156.

Tomasello, M., & Todd, J. (1983). Joint attention and lexical acquisition style. *First Language*, **4**, 197–212.

Udwin, O., & Yule, W. (1990). Expressive language of children with Williams syndrome. *American Journal of Medical Genetics Supplement*, **6**, 108–114.

Vallar, G., & Papagno, C. (1993). Preserved vocabulary acquisition in Down's syndrome: The role of phonological short-term memory. *Cortex*, **29**, 467–483.

# AUTHOR'S RESPONSE

## RESPONSE TO THE COMMENTARY BY MERVIS AND ROBINSON

*Marian Sigman*

The aims of the research described in this monograph are twofold: (1) to identify the central deficits that characterize the psychological development of children with autism and children with Down syndrome, and (2) to determine the precursors of more adequate verbal and social development of children with these neurodevelopmental disabilities. The commentary of Mervis and Robinson is focused on the methods and findings related to the first aim. Their broader argument is that the method of comparing the performance of children with different syndromes in order to identify central deficits is faulty because of difficulties in matching groups and because it does not furnish information about individuals. For this reason, they suggest an alternative technique. Their narrower point is that the deficits attributed to children with autism in this monograph may be due to differences in language abilities because the group matching on language skills was imprecise. My response to this commentary is directed at addressing the questions about group comparisons and the extent to which we have identified specific, unique, and universal deficits in autism, as well as considering the alternative measure proposed by Mervis and Robinson.

## THE ISSUE OF GROUP COMPARISONS

The identification of shared characteristics of children with a particular neurodevelopmental disability is important for several reasons. First, the understanding of the phenotype of a disorder is critical for research into its etiology. The genetic basis of Down syndrome would not have been identified if the shared physical attributes of individuals with Down syndrome had not been recognized. Second, diagnosis of disorders where the biological basis is

131

unknown depends on the use of behavioral observations and interviews to assess the critical symptoms of the disorder. Individuals with Down syndrome are diagnosed with genetic testing, whereas the diagnosis of autism depends on developmental delays in social and communicative behaviors, some of which are described in this monograph. Without an understanding of the deficits and strengths shared by children with autism, there would be no way to formulate criteria or measures for diagnosis.

The determination of specific and unique deficits requires that the group of children be compared with another group of children who do not have the disorder. When my research group and I first began our research into autism, there were many clinical descriptions of the children. However, these descriptions were largely uninformative because there was no way of knowing whether the autistic children differed from nonautistic children of the same age on the characteristics described. Even the few reports that included comparison groups did not take into account the high prevalence of mental retardation within autistic samples. Without comparisons of autistic children with nonautistic children of similar developmental level, it was not clear whether the characteristics attributed to autism were really caused by the mental retardation that accompanied the disorder. The use of comparison groups, pioneered by Hermelin & O'Connor (1970), furnished a model for research in this area and provided useful leads for future investigations.

The criticisms of Mervis and Robinson of the group comparison method are not without merit. There are no perfect comparison groups in that each group of children tends to have characteristics of its own that may affect the comparison. Mervis and Robinson give a good example of this by showing how the use of children with Down syndrome as a comparison group may affect the results of group comparisons because of the weakness in expressive language skills manifested by children with Down syndrome. We and other investigators have tried to get around this by using a comparison group of children with heterogenous developmental delays as well as a typically developing sample. The latter is useful to determine whether certain behavioral patterns characterize children with any form of developmental disabilities, regardless of the particular syndrome.

Another issue in using comparison groups is the selection of matching variables. The criteria for choosing a matching variable and the method to measure this matching variable are often ambiguous. In the early days of autism research, groups were usually matched on Performance IQ rather than on Verbal IQ or Full Scale IQ. The rationale for using Performance IQ was that this was the area of greatest strength of children with autism, although this matching meant that the Verbal IQ and Full Scale IQ of the comparison group were usually higher than the children with autism. Recent research has used matching on either overall abilities (reflected usually in mental age) or on verbal abilities (reflected usually in language age).

Groups often are matched on chronological age as well. Of course, developmentally delayed groups can never be matched on both mental age and chronological age with a typically developing group.

There are two problems involved in matching on language age. First, one of the three criteria required for the diagnosis of autism is a communication disorder, manifested in serious problems in language. Thus, children with autism generally are much less competent verbally than other children with developmental disabilities. In matching on this variable, the investigator is controlling for the defining characteristic of the disorder. To the extent that other abilities are related to language skills, group differences on these abilities will be minimized even though the abilities may be very discriminating from a diagnostic standpoint. Second, matching closely on language age usually means that the comparison groups are of lower mental and chronological ages. For both these reasons, in our past research, we have matched groups on mental age except when there were very strong justifications for matching on language age.

## CENTRAL DEFICITS IN JOINT ATTENTION, EMOTIONAL RESPONSIVENESS, AND SYMBOLIC PLAY

My research group and I have been working on defining the central deficits in autism for about 20 years. In a series of studies using samples ranging from 16 to 30 children in a group, we have compared children with autism to a mixed group of children with Down syndrome and other developmental delays and a typically developing group. In each of these studies, almost all the children were matched on an individual basis so that the members of each pair did not differ on mental age (MA) by more than 3 months or on chronological age (CA) by more than 5 months (this was not true for the typically developing children). None of the data from the children with developmental disabilities was dropped from analyses because of a failure to match although some of the data from the typically developing children were deleted for this reason. Of course, the pair-based matching resulted in groups that were matched. In two studies, the children with autism initiated joint attention and responded to bids for joint attention less than the control groups (Mundy, Sigman, & Kasari, 1994; Mundy, Sigman, Ungerer, & Sherman, 1986) and, in three studies, the children with autism looked at a distressed adult less than the control subjects (Corona, Dissanayake, Arbelle, Wellington, & Sigman, 1998; Dissanayake, Sigman, & Kasari, 1996; Sigman, Kasari, Kwon, & Yirmiya, 1992). Thus, there seemed to be a unique deficit in joint attention and emotional responsiveness in autistic children based on comparisons with data from children rather closely matched on mental and chronological ages. The results in terms of functional and symbolic play

133

were somewhat more variable in that the findings depended on whether play was assessed in an unstructured or structured setting (Mundy et al., 1986; Sigman & Ungerer, 1984).

In the current monograph, these analyses were repeated with the addition of data from a study of children with Down syndrome, children with developmental delays, and typically developing children who were somewhat younger than the subjects in the studies of children with autism. In addition, we substituted group-matching for pair-matching and language age-matching for mental age-matching. We had decided to match the children at older ages on language age because of the importance of language skills for peer interactions, a major focus of the follow-up. In order to keep the matching variable consistent throughout the monograph, language age-matching rather than mental age-matching was used for the younger children as well. Groups were considered matched on language age if the differences between them were not significant using a probability value of .101. This value was chosen because matching at a higher probability value caused the groups to differ significantly on mental age so that the children with autism had higher mental ages than the other groups. In addition, we wanted to drop as little of the data as possible. The results supported those from the previous analyses in that the autistic children appeared to have specific, unique, and universal deficits in initiating joint attention and emotional responsiveness. The children with autism also appeared to have a specific and unique deficit in responding to bids for joint attention, although this deficit was not universal in that there were no significant group differences at the later age point. Finally, the children with autism engaged in fewer symbolic play acts although this comparison was computed with language age covaried as it was impossible to equalize the language ages of the groups assessed with this measure.

Mervis and Robinson agree that children with autism may have these deficits compared to children of the same mental age but not compared to children of the same language age because the matching on language age was not conservative enough. In addition, the children in the different groups may be at different points in their vocabulary spurt. In order to address this issue, we compared three of the four groups of children on the frequency of initiating joint attention, the percentage of responses to bids for joint attention, the duration of gazing at the distressed experimenter, and the number of symbolic play acts including only children with a language age of 14 months or less. The data from the Down syndrome sample were excluded because of difficulties in equating them on control variables as well as their lesser relevance for the differentiation of autism from other conditions. For the sample of 66 participants tested on joint attention, the mean language age was 12.53 ($SD$ = .73) for the autistic group, 12.58 ($SD$ = .79) for the developmentally delayed group, and 12.83 ($SD$ = .68) for the typically developing group with a $p = .32$. These groups are well matched on language age (particularly the autistic and developmentally delayed groups) and all the children are well before the vocabulary spurt. The groups differed significantly on the frequency of initiating joint attention, $F(2, 63) = 20.44$, $p < .0001$, and the percentage of responses to bids for joint attention, $F(2, 63) = 7.50$, $p < .001$. According to the Newman–Keuls test, the children with autism initiated joint attention significantly less than the children with developmental delays, $p < .0002$, and less than the typically developing children, $p < .0002$. The children with autism responded less to bids for joint attention than the children with developmental delays, $p < .03$, and less than the typically developing children, $p < .002$. Thus, autistic children showed less joint attention than the other two groups despite being older.

The results were similar for initiating joint attention in analyses of data from children with language ages over 14 months, although the language matching was less precise, $p = .23$. The more verbally adept groups did not differ on percentage of responses to bids for joint attention, corroborating our previous results using mental age as a matching variable (Mundy, Sigman, & Kasari, 1994), the results from the follow-up study reported in this monograph, and the findings of other investigators (Charman, 1997; DiLavore, Lord, & Rutter, 1995). The lack of group differences in more advanced groups may be because of ceiling effects in that normal and developmentally delayed children come to follow pointing gestures every time. Other possible explanations are that children with autism who are able to follow the attention of another may be more likely to acquire language or that autistic children with adequate language skills may learn to follow the attention of others.

For the sample of 37 children whose duration of gaze to the distressed experimenter was observed, the language ages of each of the three groups was 12.8, with a $p = .94$. The groups differed significantly on the duration of gaze to the distressed experimenter, $F(3, 34) = 33.96$, $p < .0001$. According to the Newman–Keuls test, the children with autism looked significantly less than the children with developmental delays, $p < .0001$, and less than the typically developing children, $p < .0001$. Thus, the children with autism also appear to be uniquely deficient in emotional responsiveness despite being older than the typically developing children and the same age as the children with developmental delays. The results were identical in analyses of the data from children with language ages over 14 months although the language matching was less precise, $p = .49$. There were no significant group differences in frequency of symbolic play when the groups were subdivided according to language level.

Given the close matching of groups on language level, the evidence seems rather compelling that the children with autism as a group have deficiencies in joint attention and emotional responsiveness. The lack of

135

matching on CA, when it occurs, does not seem like much of an issue for two reasons. First, the children with autism tend to be older than the other groups rather than younger. More important, CA is relevant only if cognitive and social skills improve as children grow older; this is unfortunately much less true for children with autism and developmental delays than for typically developing children. Of the variables described here, only the percentage of responding to bids for joint attention is correlated with CA for the children with autism.

The reservations of Mervis and Robinson about the universality of the deficits are appropriate in that there are children with autism who are not deficient in some of the characteristics that we have studied. Of course, there will be some normal children who respond less to bids for joint attention than children with autism if the mental or language age of the typically developing children is lower. Moreover, as mentioned in the monograph, children with developmental disabilities may be able to compensate for deficiencies in some areas through skills in others. An excellent example furnished by Mervis & Robinson is of children with Down syndrome whose good auditory memory seems to help them acquire good expressive language. In line with this example is the high social responsiveness of nonretarded adolescents with autism (Capps, Yirmiya, & Sigman, 1992; Yirmiya, Sigman, Kasari, & Mundy, 1992) who pay a great deal of attention to videotaped vignettes of children in emotionally upsetting situations. These children also show adequate social understanding that they seem to have acquired by using their good cognitive skills. Obviously, no single deficit is likely to be deficient in all children with autism except some form of language delay that is required for the diagnosis of the disorder, although it is not unique to the disorder of autism.

## THE PROPOSED METHOD FOR DETERMINING SPECIFIC, UNIQUE, AND UNIVERSAL CHARACTERISTICS

Because of the limitations of the group comparison measure, Mervis and Robinson propose an alternative method that does seem intriguing. However, the method of profile analysis described is not applicable to mentally retarded, autistic individuals because of their double disabilities. The method requires a measure that has been "normed" on a single sample of individuals, who would seem by this description to be normal children. Moreover, the essence of standardizing is the use of some characteristic of the norming sample, usually CA, to equalize differences in task performance found in typically developing populations as a function of age. Thus, the method proposed by Mervis & Robinson does not obviate the need for a comparison group or matching variables. Moreover, the autistic children would essentially be compared with typically developing children of the same chronological ages so that we would not know how much of the variation in scores was attributable to mental retardation and how much was attributable to autism. Perhaps the suggestion is to use "norms" for typically developing children with comparisons made not on CA but on mental or language age. However, a typically developing group of the same mental or language age is a poor comparison for an autistic group, because there might be differences in distribution of abilities as a function of developmental disorder that were not specific to autism.

The requirement is to use a scale that takes into account the developmental delay shown by most autistic individuals. Hypothetically, the measure could be "normed" on mentally retarded children, but one would then have to choose which mentally retarded group to use. Moreover, there are very few ability measures standardized on mentally retarded samples, aside from some adaptive behavior scales, as this requires very large samples of individuals with mental retardation. Another challenge is that psychometric scales of nonverbal communication or responsiveness to others' emotions need to be formulated using a conceptual framework for developmental change in these behaviors. A scale of nonverbal communication and social behaviors would apply to children functioning at less than 4 years as children who speak well no longer engage in nonverbal behaviors in the same way. Scales would need to be formulated that replace the nonverbal measures with assessments of pragmatic skills in conversation and sympathetic verbal reactions to the distress of others.

The sensitivity and specificity measures (if not the profiling measures) described by Mervis and Robinson could be applied to this sample as long as categorical rather than continuous variables were used. For example, if we considered all children with fewer than 12 initiations of joint attention to be deficient, the $Se$ of joint attention as a characteristic of autism is .78 and the $Sp$ is .74. The $Se$ and $Sp$ of responding to 50% or fewer of the bids for joint attention are .70 and .74, respectively, and the $Se$ and $Sp$ of looking at a distressed experimenter less than 40% of the time are .74 and .84, respectively.

A very promising instrument for determining $Se$ and $Sp$ is the Autism Diagnostic Observation Schedule (ADOS-G; Lord, Rutter, & DiLavore, 1998). This schedule is composed of four modules that are differentiated on the basis of the expressive language level of the subject into no speech, phrase speech, and verbal fluency (with two scales for the verbally fluent differentiated on CA). Each of about 28–30 behaviors is rated on a 3 to 4-point scale with the behaviors selected on the basis of previous findings of group differences like those described in this monograph. The ADOS-G is being administered to more than 1,000 subjects with autism and control subjects in the 10 newly organized Collaborative Programs of Excellence in Autism, funded by the National Institute of Child Health and Human Development and the National Institute of Deafness and Communication Disorders. It should be possible with this instrument to determine the specificity and sensitivity of behavioral ratings of many of the nonverbal communicative and social behaviors discussed in this monograph.

The findings from the studies of group differences reviewed in this monograph and published by others also have been utilized in research programs aimed at facilitating earlier diagnosis than is now possible. Several scales for early diagnosis have been formulated and appear to differentiate children in the second year of life who will later be diagnosed as autistic from those who will not (Baron-Cohen et al., 1996; Osterling & Dawson, 1994). Since diagnosis is always done on an individual level, the sensitivity and specificity of the components of the diagnostic scale can be evaluated.

We agree with Mervis and Robinson that the eventual aim is to determine the extent to which deficits and strengths characterize individuals who are diagnosed with a syndrome. However, in our view, group comparisons, with all their faults, are necessary for the progress needed to formulate measures that can be used with individuals. At the same time, group differences are not sufficient for directing interventions, as these may be based on individual characteristics. For this reason, our current research is less concerned with differentiating children with autism from other groups and more focused on identifying processes that account for the variation within the group so that the individual development of children with autism and with other developmental disabilities can be optimized.

## REFERENCES

Baron-Cohen, S., Cox, A., Baird, G., Sweetenham, J., Nightingale, N., Morgan, K., Drew, A., & Charman, T. (1996). Psychological markers in the detection of autism in infancy in a large population. *British Journal of Psychiatry*, **168**, 158–163.

Capps, L., Yirmiya, N., & Sigman, M. (1992). Understandings of simple and complex emotions in non-retarded children with autism. *Journal of Child Psychology and Psychiatry*, **33**, 1169–1182.

Charman, T. (1997). The relationship between joint attention and pretend play in autism. *Development and Psychopathology*, **9**, 1–16.

Corona, R., Dissanayake, C., Arbelle, S., Wellington, P., & Sigman, M. (1998). Is affect aversive to young children with autism?: Behavioral and cardiac responses to experimenter distress. *Child Development*, **69**, 1494–1502.

DiLavore, P. C., Lord, C., & Rutter, M. (1995). Pre-linguistic autism diagnostic observation schedule. *Journal of Autism and Development Disorders*, **25**, 355–379.

Dissanayake, C., Sigman, M., & Kasari, C. (1996). Long-term stability of individual differences in the emotional responsiveness of children with autism. *Journal of Child Psychology and Psychiatry*, **37**, 461–467.

Hermelin, B., & O'Connor, N. (1970). *Psychological experiments with autistic children*. New York: Pergamon Press.

Lord, C., Rutter, M., & DiLavore, P. C. (1998). *The Autism Diagnostic Observation Schedule— Generic.* Unpublished manual, University of Chicago.

Mundy, P., Sigman, M., & Kasari, C. (1994). Joint attention, developmental level and symptom presentation in autism. *Development and Psychopathology,* **6**, 389–401.

Mundy, P., Sigman, M., Ungerer, J., & Sherman, T. (1986). Defining the social deficits of autism: The contribution of nonverbal communication measures. *Journal of Child Psychology and Psychiatry,* **27**, 657–669.

Osterling, J., & Dawson, G. (1994). Early recognition of children with autism: A study of first birthday home videotapes. *Journal of Autism and Developmental Disorders,* **24**, 247–257.

Sigman, M. D., Kasari, C., Kwon, J., & Yirmiya, N. (1992). Responses to the negative emotions of others by autistic, mentally retarded, and normal children. *Child Development,* **63**, 796–807.

Sigman, M. D., & Ungerer, J. A. (1984). Cognitive and language skills in autistic, mentally retarded, and normal children. *Developmental Psychology,* **20**, 293–302.

Yirmiya, N., Sigman, M., Kasari, C., & Mundy, P. (1992). Empathy and cognition in high-functioning children with autism. *Child Development,* **63**, 150–160.

# CONTRIBUTORS

**Marian Sigman** (Ph.D. 1970, Boston University) is a Professor of Psychiatry and Psychology at UCLA. Her research concerns the development of children with disabilities and those at high risk because of mild malnutrition, preterm birth, and maternal anxiety disorders. She is coauthor with Lisa Capps of the book *Children With Autism: A Developmental Perspective*, published by Harvard University Press.

**Ellen Ruskin** (Ph.D. 1989, University of California at Los Angeles) is a Research Psychologist in the Department of Psychiatry at UCLA School of Medicine. Her research interests are focused on peer interactions and social competence in children with developmental disabilities.

**Shoshana Arbelle** (M.D. 1984, Ben Gurion Medical School) is an Associate Professor, Department of Psychiatry, Beer-Sheva University, Israel. She is particularly interested in diagnosis of children with pervasive developmental disabilities.

**Rosalie A. Corona** (M.A. 1994, University of California, Los Angeles) is a graduate student in clinical psychology at University of California, Los Angeles. Her research program spans a variety of areas including the social development of children with autism and the influence of individual, cultural, and family processes on the psychosocial adjustment of Latino adolescents.

**Cheryl Dissanayake** (Ph.D. 1992, Monash University) is a Lecturer in Applied Psychology at La Trobe University, Melbourne, Australia. She has carried out a number of studies on attachment behaviors in children with autism and is currently contrasting the development of individuals with Asperger's syndrome and individuals with autism.

**Michael Espinosa** (Ph.D. 1991, University of California, Los Angeles) is a Research Psychologist in the Departments of Psychiatry and Pediatrics at the UCLA School of Medicine. His research aims at identifying the effects of early intervention with children at risk because of maternal drug use, preterm birth, poverty, and chronic malnutrition.

**Norman Kim** (M.A. 1997, University of California, Los Angeles) is a graduate student in clinical psychology at University of California, Los Angeles. His dissertation is a study of fMRI in autistic adults in response to affectively arousing stimuli.

**Alma R. López** (B.A. 1995, University of California, Los Angeles) is a graduate student in clinical psychology at California State University, Northridge. She is interested in social communication and play in children with autism and other developmental disabilities and the cultural influences on children's social and emotional development.

**Cynthia Zierhut** (B.A. 1992, University of Colorado) is a graduate student in developmental psychology at the University of California at Los Angeles. She is currently involved in observational studies of caregiver interactions with young children with autism.

**Carolyn B. Mervis** (Ph.D., 1976, Cornell University) is professor of psychology and distinguished university scholar at the University of Louisville. Her research interests are focused on language acquisition and cognitive development. Much of her current work compares and contrasts the early development of children who are developing normally, children who have Williams syndrome, and children who have Down syndrome. She is on the editorial board of *American Journal of Mental Retardation*.

**Byron F. Robinson** (Ph.D., 1999, Emory University) is a research associate at the University of Louisville. He is coauthor (with Roger Bakeman) of *Understanding Log-Linear Analysis with ILOG: An Interactive Approach*, and serves on the editorial board of *Infancy*. His research interests focus on early language and cognitive development, behavioral genetics, and research methodology.

# STATEMENT OF EDITORIAL POLICY

The *Monographs* series is intended as an outlet for major reports of developmental research that generate authoritative new findings and use these to foster a fresh and/or better-integrated perspective on some conceptually significant issue or controversy. Submissions from programmatic research projects are particularly welcome; these may consist of individually or group-authored reports of findings from some single large-scale investigation or of a sequence of experiments centering on some particular question. Multiauthored sets of independent studies that center on the same underlying question can also be appropriate; a critical requirement in such instances is that the various authors address common issues and that the contribution arising from the set as a whole be both unique and substantial. In essence, irrespective of how it may be framed, any work that contributes significant data and/or extends developmental thinking will be taken under editorial consideration.

Submissions should contain a minimum of 80 manuscript pages (including tables and references); the upper limit of 150–175 pages is much more flexible (please submit four copies; a copy of every submission and associated correspondence is deposited eventually in the archives of the SRCD). Neither membership in the Society for Research in Child Development nor affiliation with the academic discipline of psychology are relevant; the significance of the work in extending developmental theory and in contributing new empirical information is by far the most crucial consideration. Because the aim of the series is not only to advance knowledge on specialized topics but also to enhance cross-fertilization among disciplines or subfields, it is important that the links between the specific issues under study and larger questions relating to developmental processes emerge as clearly to the general reader as to specialists on the given topic.

Potential authors who may be unsure whether the manuscript they are planning would make an appropriate submission are invited to draft an outline of what they propose and send it to the Editor for assessment. This mechanism, as well as a more detailed desctiption of all editorial policies, evaluation processes, and format requirements, is given in the "Guidelines for the Preparation of *Monographs* Submissions," which can be obtained by contacting the Editor Elect, Willis Overton, Department of Psychology, 567 Weiss Hall, Temple University, Philadelphia, PA 19122 (e-mail: overton@vm.temple.edu).